EXPLORING ENZYMES

NATURE'S CATALYST

JITENDRA KUMAR
SHOEB AHMED

This book, *Exploring Enzyme: Nature's Catalyst*, is dedicated to the inquisitive minds of undergraduate students embarking on their journey into the fascinating world of enzymology. May it serve as a guiding light to inspire curiosity, foster understanding, and ignite a lifelong passion for the science of enzymes.

To all the teachers and mentors who nurture the love for learning, and to the students who push the boundaries of knowledge—this book is for you.

Contents

Foreword

Enzymes, often referred to as nature's catalysts, are central to the biochemical processes that sustain life. They govern a wide range of reactions with remarkable precision, from the breakdown of nutrients in our bodies to the synthesis of complex molecules essential for survival. Understanding how enzymes function is critical for students pursuing careers in the biological and biochemical sciences, as it lays the foundation for fields such as medicine, biotechnology, and environmental science.

Exploring Enzyme: Nature's Catalyst is designed to introduce the fundamentals of enzymology to undergraduate students. This book offers a comprehensive yet accessible approach to the core concepts of enzyme structure, function, kinetics, and regulation. With a clear focus on making enzymology approachable, it bridges the gap between theoretical knowledge and real-world applications, helping students appreciate the relevance of enzymes in biological systems.

What sets this book apart is its emphasis on clarity, simplicity, and real-life examples, ensuring that students not only grasp the fundamental principles but also develop a genuine interest in the subject. The step-by-step explanations of complex mechanisms, supported by diagrams and illustrations, make even the most challenging topics easy to comprehend.

Whether you are a student beginning your journey into the world of biochemistry or an educator seeking a reliable resource to guide your teaching, *Exploring Enzyme: Nature's Catalyst* will serve as a valuable tool in understanding the fascinating dynamics of enzymes. I do not doubt that this book will inspire a new generation of students to explore the limitless possibilities within enzymology.

Preface

Enzymes are at the heart of all biological reactions, driving processes essential to life with remarkable efficiency and specificity. As students of the life sciences, gaining a thorough understanding of how enzymes function is crucial to mastering the fundamentals of biochemistry, molecular biology, and biotechnology. It is with this in mind that *Exploring Enzyme: Nature's Catalyst* has been written, aiming to introduce the essential principles of enzymology to undergraduate students.

This book is crafted to offer an accessible entry point into the field of enzymology. The content is structured to provide clear, concise explanations of enzyme mechanisms, kinetics, and regulation, with a focus on making complex topics approachable. Every effort has been made to ensure that the material is presented in a way that encourages active learning and fosters a deeper appreciation for the role of enzymes in both natural and applied biological processes.

Throughout the chapters, real-world examples and illustrations have been included to bridge theory with practice, helping students relate the core concepts to practical applications in biotechnology, medicine, agriculture, and industry. This approach is intended to not only build a solid foundational knowledge of enzymology but also to inspire students to think critically about how enzymes shape the world around us.

The goal of *Exploring Enzyme: Nature's Catalyst* is to equip undergraduate students with the essential tools to confidently navigate the complexities of enzymology, preparing them for advanced studies and careers in the biological sciences. We hope that this book serves as both a learning guide and a source of inspiration, encouraging students to delve deeper into the wonders of enzyme science.

Author: **Dr. Jitendra Kumar**

Co-Author: **Shoeb Ahmed**

Acknowledgements

Writing *Exploring Enzyme: Nature's Catalyst* has been a deeply rewarding journey, and this book would not have been possible without the support, guidance, and encouragement of many individuals.

First and foremost, we would like to express our heartfelt gratitude to all the teachers and mentors who have inspired and nurtured our passion for science, especially enzymology. Their dedication to teaching and commitment to fostering curiosity in their students has been a constant source of motivation.

A special thanks to our colleagues and peers who generously shared their knowledge and provided valuable feedback during the development of this book. Their insights have greatly enriched the content and helped shape it into a resource that we hope will benefit students for years to come.

We are also deeply grateful to our family and friends, whose unwavering support has been a pillar of strength throughout this endeavour. Their encouragement and patience made the long hours of writing and revising much more manageable.

Finally, to the students who will be using this book, we acknowledge your enthusiasm and curiosity. Your desire to learn and explore truly inspired me to create this work. We hope this book helps illuminate the fascinating world of enzymes and serves as a stepping stone in your academic and scientific journey.

Thank you all for being part of this project, directly or indirectly. Your contributions and support have made this book a reality.

Author: **Dr. Jitendra Kumar**

Co-Author: **Shoeb Ahmed**

Prologue

Enzymes are the unseen architects of life, orchestrating the biochemical reactions that sustain every living organism. Their ability to accelerate chemical reactions with precision and control has fascinated scientists for centuries, leading to groundbreaking discoveries that have revolutionized medicine, agriculture, and biotechnology. Yet, for many students, the study of enzymes can initially seem daunting, given the complexity of their mechanisms and the intricacies of the reactions they govern.

Exploring Enzyme: Nature's Catalyst was born out of a desire to demystify enzymology and present it in a way that is both engaging and comprehensible for undergraduate students. This book is not just a textbook; it is a gateway to understanding the fascinating world of enzymes, a field that holds the key to many of today's most important scientific advancements.

In the chapters that follow, we will journey through the essential concepts of enzymology, from the fundamental principles of enzyme structure and function to the kinetics that defines their behaviour. We will explore how enzymes catalyse reactions with incredible speed and specificity, and how their regulation is critical to maintaining life's delicate balance. Through a combination of clear explanations, diagrams, and practical examples, this book aims to make the complex world of enzymes accessible to all.

As you turn the pages of *Exploring Enzyme: Nature's Catalyst*, We hope you will not only gain a solid foundation in the science of enzymes but also develop a curiosity and appreciation for the vital role they play in both nature and technology. May this book inspire you to explore further, question deeper, and contribute to the ever-expanding understanding of these remarkable biological catalysts.

Author: **Dr. Jitendra Kumar**

Co-Author: **Shoeb Ahmed**

CHAPTER I

Introduction to Enzymes

What are Enzymes?

Enzymes are highly specialized biological catalysts, primarily composed of proteins, that accelerate biochemical reactions essential for sustaining life within living organisms. These molecular machines operate with remarkable efficiency, facilitating specific chemical transformations by lowering the activation energy required for reactions, thereby increasing reaction rates by up to a million times compared to non-catalysed processes. This ability to operate under mild conditions of temperature and pH, often within narrow ranges, is crucial for maintaining the orderly and regulated metabolic pathways necessary for life. Structurally, enzymes are composed of one or more polypeptide chains that fold into unique three-dimensional shapes, forming active sites where substrate molecules bind. This binding induces a conformational change in the enzyme, which facilitates the conversion of substrates into products. The specificity of enzymes, which follows models like the "lock and key" or "induced fit" hypothesis, ensures that they catalysed only one particular type of chemical reaction among many possible in a cell, thereby preventing metabolic chaos. This high selectivity and regulation by factors such as temperature, pH, substrate concentration, and regulatory molecules allow enzymes to efficiently drive vital processes such as digestion, respiration, energy production, and the synthesis of essential molecules like proteins, nucleic acids, and carbohydrates. Additionally, some enzymes are composed of RNA molecules, known as ribozymes, which also exhibit catalytic activity. The unique sequence and arrangement of amino acids or nucleotides within enzymes determine their catalytic properties and substrate specificity, allowing them to function with remarkable precision. Overall, enzymes are indispensable components of biological systems, driving the myriads of biochemical reactions necessary for life to thrive, and ensuring the maintenance of overall health and homeostasis.

Definitions of Enzymes

Enzymes, the biological catalysts fundamental to life processes, have been defined in various ways by scientists and institutions, reflecting their critical role in biochemical reactions. Different definitions of enzymes are

1

given here:

- **International Union of Biochemistry and Molecular Biology (IUBMB)**: "Enzymes are biological catalysts that accelerate chemical reactions in living organisms. They are typically proteins that bind to specific substrates and convert them into products by lowering the activation energy of the reaction."
- **Enzyme Commission (EC)**: "Enzymes are proteins or RNA molecules that catalysed biochemical reactions by providing an alternative reaction pathway with a lower activation energy, thus increasing the rate of the reaction."
- **Albert L. Lehninger (Biochemist)**: "Enzymes are high-molecular-weight proteins that act as biological catalysts. They speed up chemical reactions by providing an environment that lowers the activation energy required for the reaction to proceed."
- **Jeremy M. Berg, John L. Tymoczko, and Lubert Stryer (Authors of 'Biochemistry')**: "Enzymes are biological molecules, predominantly proteins, that act as catalysts to increase the rates of chemical reactions without being consumed or permanently altered in the process."
- **David L. Nelson and Michael M. Cox (Authors of 'Lehninger Principles of Biochemistry')**: "Enzymes are specialized proteins that accelerate chemical reactions in living systems by lowering the activation energy of the reaction, making it possible for the reaction to proceed at a much faster rate."
- **Molecular Cell Biology Textbooks**: "Enzymes are catalytic proteins that facilitate biochemical reactions by lowering the activation energy and increasing the rate of the reaction. They are specific to their substrates and often operate within complex cellular pathways."
- **Biochemical Society**: "Enzymes are biomolecules that serve as catalysts to accelerate chemical reactions in biological systems. They do so by binding to substrates and converting them into products through a series of intermediates."
- **Harper's Illustrated Biochemistry**: "Enzymes are highly specific biological catalysts that speed up metabolic reactions in living organisms by lowering the activation energy necessary for the reaction to occur."

CHAPTER II

History of Enzymes

Our understanding of biological processes and the evolution of biochemistry are closely tied to the history of enzymes. The study of enzymes has significantly influenced biochemistry for much of its history, beginning with the identification of biological catalysis in stomach secretions in the late 1700s. In the 1800s, researchers conducted studies on saliva and plant extracts, observing their ability to convert starch into sugar. In the 1850s, **Louis Pasteur** concluded that "ferments" catalyse the conversion of sugar to alcohol by yeast, proposing that these ferments were intricately linked to the structure of living yeast cells. The scientific study of enzymes truly began in the early 19th century, with **Anselme Payen** and **Jean-François Persoz** isolating the first enzyme, diastase, in 1833. This discovery laid the groundwork for enzymology as a distinct scientific field. **Wilhelm Kühne** introduced the term "enzyme" in 1878, derived from the Greek "enzyme," meaning "in yeast." A major breakthrough came in 1897 when **Eduard Buchner** demonstrated that cell-free yeast extracts could ferment sugar, proving that enzymes could function outside living cells and challenging the concept of vitalism. The 20th century marked further advances, with **James B. Sumner's** crystallization of urease in 1926, confirming that enzymes are proteins. Subsequent crystallization of enzymes like pepsin and trypsin by **John Northrop** and **Wendell Stanley** solidified the understanding of enzymes as proteinaceous catalysts, paving the way for detailed structural studies. These milestones underscore the vital role enzymes have played in shaping our knowledge of biological processes and biochemistry, reflecting their essential function in life itself.

2.1. Pepsin discovery (1836):

In the early 19th century, the study of enzymes gained significant momentum with the work of **Theodor Schwann** and **Friedrich Kühne**, who discovered pepsin, an enzyme crucial for protein digestion in the stomach. Pepsin plays a vital role in breaking down proteins into peptides, facilitating their subsequent digestion and absorption. This discovery marked a pivotal point in enzymology, establishing pepsin as one of the first enzymes to be studied in detail and setting the stage for further research into enzymatic processes. Schwann and Kühne's identification of pepsin laid the foundation for the scientific exploration of enzymes, highlighting their essential role in biological digestion and advancing the field of biochemistry.

2.2. Term "enzyme" (1878):

In 1878, **Wilhelm Kühne**, a German scientist, introduced the term "enzyme" to describe the biological molecules that catalyse specific chemical reactions within organisms. Derived from the Greek words "en" (meaning "in") and "zyme" (meaning "leaven" or "yeast"), the term reflects its origins in the study of fermentation and digestion. Kühne coined the term during his research into how these catalysts facilitate biological processes, significantly advancing the concept of enzymes as biological catalysts. His work not only introduced the term but also laid the groundwork for the scientific understanding of enzymes, which has since become a cornerstone of biochemistry. The concept of enzymes as essential biological catalysts has gained widespread acceptance and remains fundamental to our understanding of metabolic processes.

2.3. Amylase (1833) & Invertase (1881) identification:

In 1833, **Anselme Payen** and **Jean-François Persoz** made a groundbreaking discovery by identifying the enzyme amylase, which plays a crucial role in converting starch into sugars. This discovery was foundational in the field of enzymology, as it demonstrated the catalytic power of enzymes in breaking down complex carbohydrates. Later, in 1881, the enzyme invertase was discovered, which is responsible for hydrolysing sucrose into glucose and fructose. Both of these enzymes significantly advanced the understanding of enzymatic functions and contributed to the development of biochemistry by elucidating how enzymes facilitate essential biochemical transformations.

2.4. Kinetics of enzyme (1902-1913):

In 1902, **Leonor Michaelis** and **Maud Menten** developed the Michaelis-Menten equation, a fundamental contribution to enzymology that explains the kinetics of enzyme-catalysed reactions. This equation elucidates the relationship between substrate concentration and enzyme activity, offering a quantitative framework for understanding how enzymes work. Michaelis and Menten's collaborative research led to the formulation of this essential equation, which remains a cornerstone in the study of enzyme kinetics. Their influential paper, *Die Kinetik der Invertin Wirkung*, published in *Biochemische Zeitschrift* in 1913, celebrates its centennial this year, marking a significant milestone in the history of enzymology.

2.5. Nobel Prize for enzymes in Chemistry (1926):

In 1926, **James B. Sumner** achieved a significant milestone by isolating and crystallizing urease, becoming the first to successfully purify an enzyme in crystalline form. This breakthrough confirmed that enzymes are proteins and marked a major advancement in enzymology. Sumner's work, along with the contributions of **John Northrop** and **Wendell Stanley**—who also made substantial strides in enzyme research—was recognized with the Nobel Prize in Chemistry, which they shared. Their collective achievements provided critical insights into the nature and function of enzymes, laying the foundation for future developments in the field.

2.6. Coenzymes identification (1930s-1940s):

William Young and **Sir Arthur Harden** were pioneers in proposing the concept of coenzymes—essential cofactors required for enzyme activity. Their work laid the groundwork for understanding how coenzymes such as coenzyme A and NAD facilitate enzymatic reactions. The significance of coenzymes in enzyme function was further highlighted by **Fritz Albert Lipmann's** discovery of coenzyme A, which earned him the Nobel Prize in Physiology or Medicine in 1953. This discovery advanced our understanding of enzymatic mechanisms and underscored the crucial role of coenzymes in biological processes.

2.7. DNA Polymerase discovery (1956):

Arthur Kornberg's discovery of DNA polymerase, an enzyme crucial for DNA replication, marked a pivotal moment in molecular biology. This breakthrough was instrumental in advancing the study of genetic information transfer and opened new avenues for understanding the mechanisms underlying genetic processes. Kornberg, along with Spanish scientist and physician **Severo Ochoa**, was awarded the Nobel Prize in Physiology or Medicine in 1959 for their work on "the mechanisms in the biological synthesis of ribonucleic acid and deoxyribonucleic acid." Their discoveries significantly contributed to our understanding of nucleic acid synthesis and solidified their impact on the field of molecular biology.

2.8. Recombinant DNA Technology (1970s):

The advancement of recombinant DNA technology in the 1970s marked a significant breakthrough in biotechnology, driven by key scientific contributions. **Paul Berg** pioneered this field by creating the first recombinant DNA molecules in 1972, demonstrating the feasibility of combining DNA from different sources. **Herbert Boyer** and **Stanley Cohen** furthered this progress in 1973 by developing methods to clone genes using recombinant plasmids, enabling large-scale production of specific proteins.

Additionally, **Walter Gilbert** and **Frederick Sanger** advanced DNA sequencing techniques, which were crucial for reading and interpreting genetic codes. Collectively, their work transformed enzyme engineering and biotechnology, facilitating the large-scale manufacture of enzymes and leading to groundbreaking applications in medicine, agriculture, and industry.

2.9. Engineering of enzyme (1980s):

In the 1980s, the emergence of enzyme engineering revolutionized the design and modification of enzymes for industrial and medicinal applications, thanks to advancements in recombinant DNA technology. **Frances Arnold** played a pivotal role with her development of directed evolution, a technique that mimics natural selection to evolve enzymes with enhanced or novel properties, which has greatly benefited industrial biocatalysis and pharmaceuticals. Additionally, Stuart Schreiber contributed significantly by using chemical libraries and high-throughput screening to identify and optimize enzyme inhibitors and modulators, aiding drug discovery and therapeutic development. These innovations in protein engineering and directed evolution have expanded the capabilities of enzyme engineering, leading to tailored enzymes with specific applications and advancing the field of biotechnology and medicine.

2.10. Era of genomic (1990s-Present):

The era of genomics, spanning from the 1990s to the present, has profoundly impacted the study and application of enzymes, largely due to the completion of the Human Genome Project and advancements in genomics. The Human Genome Project, completed in 2003, provided a comprehensive map of the human genome, offering invaluable insights into the genes encoding various enzymes and their functions. This monumental achievement was spearheaded by a collaborative effort involving numerous scientists and institutions worldwide, including key figures like **Francis Collins**, who led the National Human Genome Research Institute, and **Craig Venter**, who headed the Celera Genomics team. Their work not only elucidated the genetic basis of enzyme functions but also facilitated the identification of new enzymes with potential applications in medicine and industry.

Further advancements in the field were driven by the rise of proteomics, which focuses on the large-scale study of proteins, including enzymes. Pioneering researchers like **Ruedi Aebersold** and **Mann Matthias** have made significant contributions to the development of proteomics technologies, such as mass spectrometry, which have enabled the detailed analysis of enzyme structures, functions, and interactions. These technologies have accelerated the discovery of novel enzymes and provided deeper insights into their roles in various biological processes.

The integration of genomics and proteomics has transformed our understanding of enzyme biology, leading to the discovery of previously unknown enzymes and enhancing our ability to engineer and apply these biological catalysts in diverse fields. This era has not only expanded the knowledge of enzyme structure and function but has also paved the way for innovations in drug development, disease research, and biotechnology.

CHAPTER III

Characteristics of Enzymes

Enzymes are biological molecules that act as catalysts, accelerating and facilitating chemical reactions essential for sustaining life. They are integral to numerous metabolic processes, each performing specific functions based on their unique structures. The primary structure of an enzyme is determined by the sequence of amino acids in its polypeptide chain. This primary sequence folds into secondary, tertiary, and sometimes quaternary structures, which are crucial for the enzyme's functionality. Understanding these structural levels is vital for comprehending how enzymes catalysed reactions, regulate physiological processes, and exhibit substrate specificity. Enzymes' ability to influence biochemical pathways and their precise regulation underscore their importance in the survival and proper functioning of organisms. Therefore, elucidating enzyme structures is key to unravelling their mechanisms and optimizing their applications in various biological and industrial contexts.

Characteristics of enzymes include:

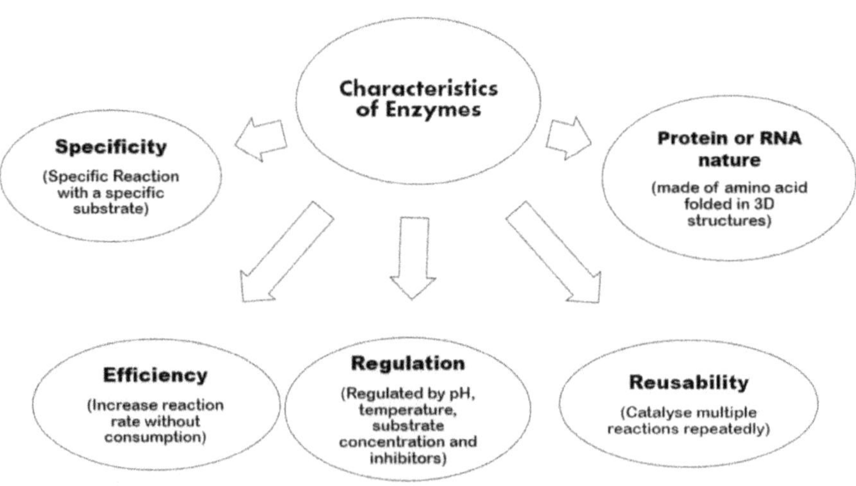

Figure 1 Characteristics of enzymes

3.1 Specificity:

Enzyme specificity is crucial for the accurate and efficient catalysis of biochemical processes in living organisms. This specificity arises from the unique arrangement of amino acids in the enzyme's active site, which creates a highly selective chemical environment tailored to a particular substrate. Enzymes bind to specific substrates with high affinity, effectively excluding molecules that do not match the active site's precise configuration. This selectivity is not only determined by the shape of the active site but also by the specific interactions between the functional groups of both the enzyme and the substrate, as well as the physical proximity of these groups during catalysis. The three-dimensional structure of the enzyme is complementary to the transition state of the reaction, which further enhances specificity by stabilizing only the appropriate substrates while excluding non-substrates from inducing the necessary conformational changes for catalysis. This precise substrate recognition and catalysis is essential for maintaining the order and efficiency of metabolic pathways, thereby ensuring the proper functioning of cellular processes.

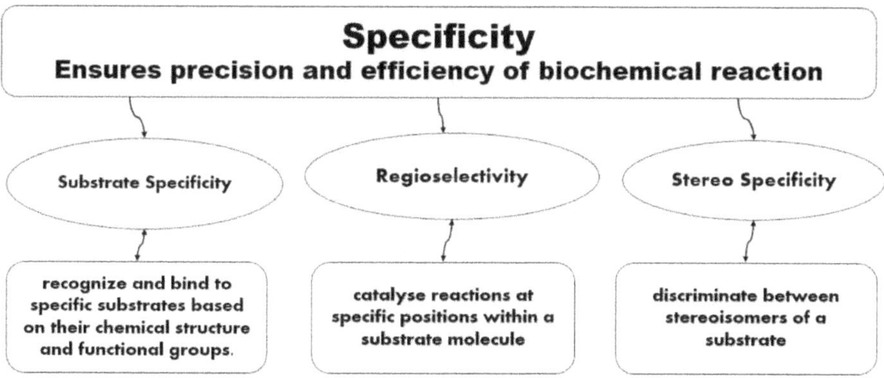

Figure 2 Specificity and its forms

Some examples of enzyme specificity are given in Table 1.

Table 1 Examples of specificity of enzymes

Specificity	Enzyme	Substrate	Reaction
Substrate	Chymotrypsin	Tryptophan, phenylalanine, and tyrosine are examples of aromatic amino acids with peptide bonds on their carboxyl side.	Peptide bonds in proteins are preferentially broken by chymotrypsin after aromatic amino acids.
Stereochemistry	Lactate Dehydrogenase	Pyruvic acid (D-lactate) or Lactic acid (L-lactate)	The interconversion of pyruvic acid and lactic acid is catalysed by lactate dehydrogenase, which exhibits stereochemistry specificity for either the L or D form of the substrate.
Regioselectivity	Cytochrome P450	Fatty acids, xenobiotics, and other medicines.	The cytochrome P450 enzymes are well-known for their ability to selectively oxidise particular carbon atoms found in organic compounds, and they frequently have an impact on medicine metabolism.
Enzyme class	Serine Protease Class (Trypsin, Elastase, Chymotrypsin)	Peptide bonds in proteins	Based on the amino acid residues close to the peptide bond it cleaves, each enzyme in the serine protease class has unique substrate specificity.
Co-factor	Alcohol Dehydrogenase	Alcohols	Nicotinamide adenine dinucleotide (NAD^+) or nicotinamide adenine dinucleotide phosphate ($NADP^+$) is a co-factor that is used by alcohol dehydrogenase to catalyse the oxidation of alcohols to aldehydes or ketones.
Temperature and pH	Pepsin	Peptide bonds in proteins	Under low pH levels, pepsin is specialised for cleaving peptide bonds at particular amino acid residues and is active in the stomach acidic environment.
DNA Polymerase	DNA Polymerase I	DNA nucleotides	During DNA replication and repair, DNA Polymerase I catalyses the synthesis of DNA by incorporating complementary nucleotides into the expanding DNA strand.
RNA Polymerase	RNA Polymerase II	Ribonucleotides	The transcription of mRNA from DNA templates is carried out by RNA Polymerase II.

3.2 Efficiency:

Enzyme efficiency is a remarkable characteristic that sets enzymes apart as highly effective catalysts in biological systems. Enzymes significantly accelerate the rate of chemical reactions without being consumed or permanently altered in the process, allowing them to function repeatedly in multiple reaction cycles. This efficiency is crucial for the rapid and precise control of biochemical processes within living organisms, enabling reactions to occur at rates that sustain life. Enzymes achieve this by lowering the activation energy required for reactions, which not only speeds up the reaction but also ensures that it occurs under the mild conditions typical of biological environments. Recent studies highlight that enzymes are not only efficient in their natural biological roles but can also be engineered for industrial applications, offering environmentally friendly alternatives to chemical catalysts. The integration of enzymatic catalysis into industrial processes underscores their potential for widespread use in sustainable technology, emphasizing the ongoing relevance and importance of enzyme efficiency in both natural and engineered contexts.

3.3 Regulation:

Enzyme activity is tightly regulated by various factors to ensure proper functioning within biological systems, allowing cells to adapt to changing environmental conditions and metabolic demands while maintaining homeostasis. Key regulatory mechanisms include allosteric regulation, where molecules bind to sites other than the active site to activate or inhibit enzyme activity, and covalent modifications such as phosphorylation, which alter enzyme function by changing its structure. Feedback inhibition prevents the overproduction of metabolic products by using the end product to inhibit early pathway enzymes. Substrate availability also influences enzyme activity, with higher concentrations typically increasing activity until the enzyme becomes saturated. Environmental factors like temperature and pH, as well as specific inhibitors and activators, further modulate enzyme activity, ensuring precise control of biochemical reactions within cells. Different factors regulating enzyme activity are depicted in Figure 3.

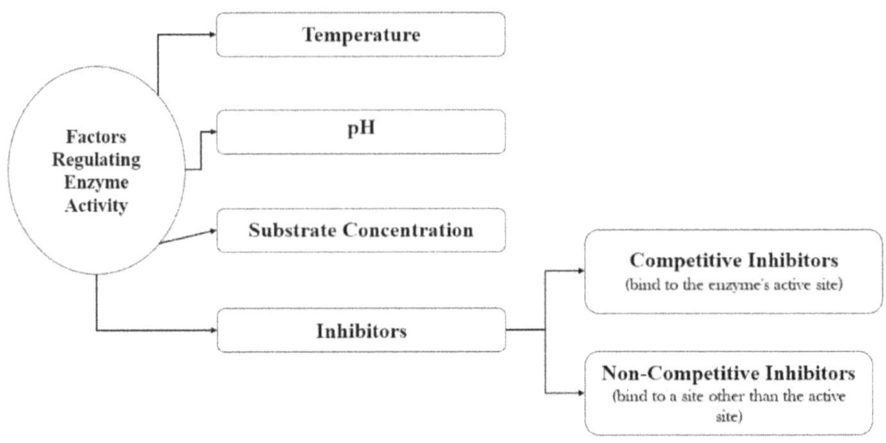

Figure 3 Factors regulating enzyme activity

3.4 Reusability:

One of the remarkable features of enzymes is their reusability, allowing them to catalysed multiple reactions repeatedly without being consumed or permanently altered in the process. This property is crucial for their effectiveness as biological catalysts and underpins their widespread use in various industrial, medical, and biotechnological applications. The reusability of enzymes is largely attributed to their inherent stability and specificity, as well as the nature of enzyme-catalysed reactions. Advances in enzyme immobilization techniques, such as ***cross-linked enzyme aggregates*** (CLEAs) and nanomaterial supports, have further enhanced the reusability and stability of enzymes, making them even more cost-effective and efficient for industrial processes. For example, immobilized enzymes on nano inorganic supports have demonstrated improved thermal and pH stability, as well as a significant increase in operational cycles, thus extending their usability in harsh industrial conditions. This reusability not only reduces the cost of enzyme production but also enhances the sustainability of biocatalytic processes, reinforcing the value of enzymes in modern applications.

3.5 Protein Nature:

Enzymes are primarily composed of proteins, which consist of linear chains of amino acids folded into specific three-dimensional structures.

This intricate proteinaceous nature is fundamental to the function and activity of enzymes, as it directly influences their catalytic properties, substrate specificity, and overall stability. The precise spatial arrangement of amino acids within the enzyme's structure creates an active site that binds substrates with high specificity, facilitating the chemical reactions necessary for life. Recent research highlights the remarkable ability of enzymes to maintain their structural integrity and functionality under various conditions, making them highly efficient biological catalysts. This efficiency is further enhanced by their ability to evolve diverse biochemical activities while retaining a common structural scaffold, allowing enzymes to adapt to different substrates and reaction conditions. This adaptability and specificity are crucial for their role in regulating complex metabolic pathways and ensuring the proper functioning of biological systems.

3.6 Enzymes are Biological Catalysts:

Enzymes are very effective biological catalysts that increase the rate of chemical reactions without consuming materials or changing the system permanently. They preserve the balance of the cellular environment by allowing reactions to take place in moderate conditions. There are some important enzymes involved in different reactions are mentioned in Table 2.

Table 2. List of important enzymes involved in different reactions

Enzyme	Substrate	Reaction
Amylase	Starch	Starch is hydrolyzed by amylase into smaller carbohydrates like glucose and maltose. Pancreatic secretions and saliva contain it.
Catalase	Hydrogen peroxide (H_2O_2)	Hydrogen peroxide is broken down into water and oxygen by catalase. Hydrogen peroxide is a byproduct of several metabolic processes, and this enzyme is essential for its detoxification.
DNA polymerase	DNA nucleotides	During DNA replication, DNA polymerase catalyses the synthesis of a new DNA strand. Complementary nucleotides are added to the expanding DNA chain by it.
RNA polymerase	RNA nucleotides	During transcription, RNA polymerase catalyses the synthesis of RNA from a DNA template. It contributes to the synthesis of other RNA molecules, including tRNA and mRNA.
Lactase	Lactose (a sugar found in milk)	Lactose is hydrolyzed into glucose and galactose by the enzyme lactase. Lactose intolerance is caused by insufficient lactase, which makes it difficult for the body to digest lactose.
ATP synthase	ADP (adenosine diphosphate) and inorganic phosphate (Pi)	ATP synthase is responsible for catalysing the synthesis of ATP from ADP and Pi in the inner mitochondrial membrane during oxidative phosphorylation.
Ribonuclease	RNA	The hydrolysis of RNA into its component nucleotides is catalysed by ribonuclease. It contributes to the turnover and destruction of RNA.
Trypsin	Proteins	Peptide bond hydrolysis in proteins is catalysed by the protease trypsin. The lysine and arginine residues' carboxyl side is the unique peptide bond that it breaks.
Hexokinase	Glucose	The phosphorylation of glucose to glucose-6-phosphate is catalysed by hexokinase. It is an initial enzyme in the process of glycolysis.
Taq polymerase (PCR enzyme)	DNA nucleotides	By amplifying particular DNA sequences, PCR enzymes like Taq polymerase catalyse the production of DNA in vitro. This is extensively utilised for DNA replication in molecular biology.

3.7 Other Features of Enzymes

Enzymes possess several other specialized features that facilitate their catalytic functions. Each enzyme contains an active site, a unique pocket or cleft with amino acid side chains that form a three-dimensional surface complementary to the substrate, enabling the formation of an enzyme-substrate (ES) complex. This complex undergoes conversion to enzyme-product (EP), which then dissociates into the enzyme and the product. Some enzymes require nonprotein cofactors—either metal ions (like Zn^{2+} ,

Fe^{2+}) or organic molecules known as coenzymes (e.g., NAD, FAD, coenzyme A)—to be active, and together, the enzyme and its cofactor are termed a holoenzyme, while the protein portion alone is known as the apoenzyme. In the absence of the cofactor, the apoenzyme generally lacks biological activity. Additionally, some enzymes feature a prosthetic group, a tightly bound coenzyme that remains attached to the enzyme. Enzymes can also have allosteric sites where effectors bind noncovalently, altering the enzyme's affinity for its substrate or its catalytic activity. Effectors that inhibit activity are called negative effectors, while those that enhance it are positive effectors. Finally, zymogens are inactive enzyme precursors that become active only after specific modifications; these are often proteolytic enzymes and are typically named with the suffix "-ogen" or the prefix "pro-".

These diverse features highlight the complex regulation and activation mechanisms that underpin enzyme functionality, reflecting their critical role in biological processes.

CHAPTER IV

Enzyme Structure

The structure of enzymes is fundamental to their function as biological catalysts, facilitating a myriad of biochemical reactions essential for life. Enzymes are complex proteins with intricate three-dimensional structures that enable them to interact specifically with their substrates. Their functional architecture typically includes an active site—a specialized region where substrate binding and catalysis occur—surrounded by a supporting framework of secondary and tertiary structures. This precise configuration allows enzymes to lower the activation energy of reactions, thereby accelerating the rate at which biochemical processes occur. Understanding enzyme structure is crucial for elucidating how enzymes work, designing inhibitors or activators, and applying this knowledge to fields such as drug development, biotechnology, and metabolic engineering.

4.1 Basics of Protein Structure

4.1.1 Primary Structure:

The primary structure of a protein (Figure 1) is the most fundamental level of its structural organization, representing the linear sequence of amino acids that make up the polypeptide chain. This sequence is determined by the arrangement of nucleotides in the gene encoding the protein, adhering to the genetic code. Each amino acid in the chain is linked by peptide bonds, forming a continuous polypeptide backbone. The specific sequence of amino acids in the primary structure dictates the protein's overall structure and function, as it influences the subsequent folding and interactions that occur in higher levels of structural organization. The primary structure is thus crucial in determining the protein's three-dimensional shape and its functional properties. Understanding this basic level of protein structure is essential for comprehending how proteins achieve their complex forms and perform their biological roles, including enzyme catalysis, cellular signalling, and structural support.

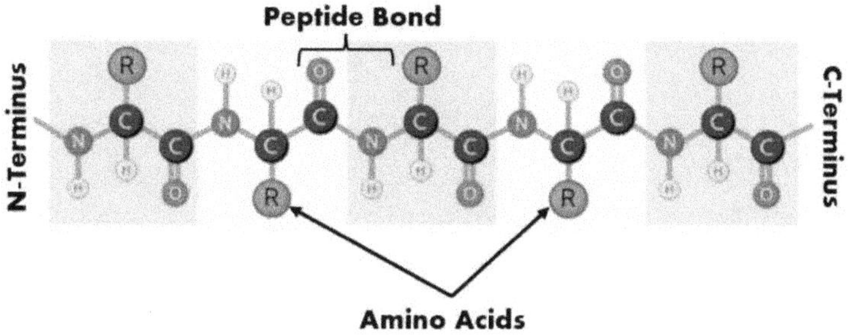

Figure 1 Primary structure of protein

4.1.1.1 Sequence of Amino Acids:

The primary structure of a protein is defined by the precise sequence of amino acids in its polypeptide chain. There are 20 standard amino acids, each with a unique side chain (R group) that imparts specific chemical properties and contributes to the protein's overall function. This sequence is determined by the order of nucleotides in the gene encoding the protein, where each set of three nucleotides, known as a codon, specifies a particular amino acid to be incorporated into the growing chain during protein synthesis. The accurate arrangement of these amino acids in the primary structure is crucial as it sets the foundation for the protein's higher-level structures and functions. The list of 20 amino acids along with their three and one-letter code is given in Table 1

Table 1 List of 20 amino acids along with their three and one-letter code

Amino Acid	Three-Letter Code	One-Letter Code
Essential		
Histidine	His	H
Isoleucine	Ile	I
Leucine	Leu	L
Lysine	Lys	K
Methionine	Met	M
Phenylalanine	Phe	F
Threonine	Thr	T
Tryptophan	Trp	W
Valine	Val	V
Arginine (semi-essential)	Arg	R
Non-Essential		
Alanine	Ala	A
Asparagine	Asn	N
Aspartic Acid	Asp	D
Cysteine	Cys	C
Glutamic Acid	Glu	E
Glutamine	Gln	Q
Glycine	Gly	G
Proline	Pro	P
Serine	Ser	S
Tyrosine	Tyr	Y

4.1.1.2. Peptide Bonds:

Peptide bonds are covalent links that connect adjacent amino acid residues within a polypeptide chain. They are formed through a condensation reaction between the amino group ($-NH_2$) of one amino acid and the carboxyl group (-COOH) of another, releasing a water molecule in the process (Figure 2). This bond has a planar structure with partial double-bond character, which restricts rotation around the bond and imparts rigidity to the polypeptide backbone. This rigidity plays a critical role in maintaining the overall stability and conformation of the protein, influencing its subsequent folding and functional properties.

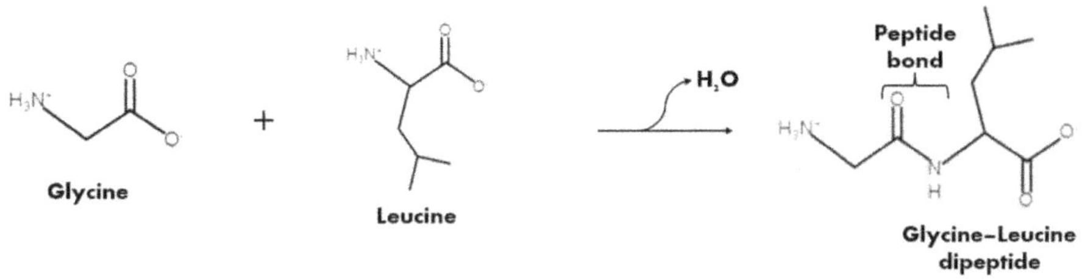

Figure 2 Reaction between glycine and leucine showing the formation of the peptide bond by the removal of the water molecule

4.1.1.3. N-terminus and C-terminus:

The primary structure of a protein is characterized by its linear sequence of amino acids, which includes two distinct termini: the N terminus and the C-terminus. The N-terminus features a free amino group ($-NH_2$) attached to the first amino acid in the chain, while the C-terminus has a free carboxyl group (-COOH) at the end of the chain (Figure 3). This structural orientation gives the polypeptide chain a defined directionality, which is conventionally described from the N-terminus to the C-terminus. The distinct ends of the polypeptide chain play crucial roles in protein synthesis and function, influencing how the protein interacts with other molecules and how it folds into its final three-dimensional structure. Understanding this directionality is fundamental for studying protein function and for applications such as protein engineering and drug design.

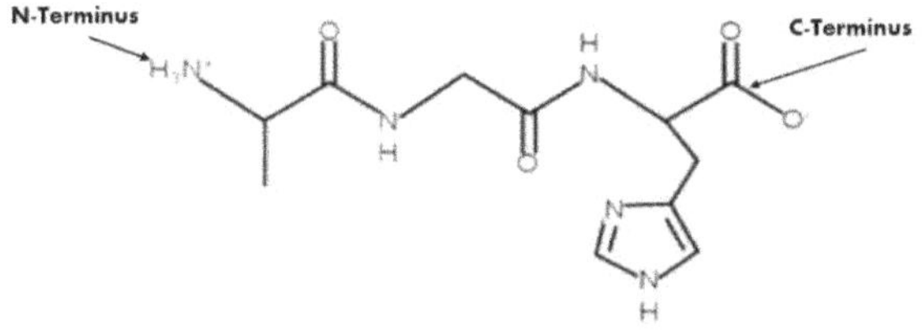

Figure 3 N terminus and C terminus depicted in alanine-glycine-histidine tripeptide

4.1.1.4. Genetic Code and Protein Synthesis:

The genetic code is a crucial set of rules that governs the translation of mRNA codons into specific amino acids during protein synthesis. Each codon, composed of three nucleotides, corresponds to one of 64 possible codons—61 of which specify amino acids (known as sense codons), and three serve as stop signals (nonsense codons) that terminate protein synthesis (Table 2). During the translation process, ribosomes decode the mRNA sequence by recognizing each codon through a complementary anticodon on a transfer RNA (tRNA) molecule, which carries the appropriate amino acid. As the ribosome moves along the mRNA, amino acids are sequentially added to the growing polypeptide chain in accordance with the mRNA sequence. This precise decoding and assembly process ensures the correct formation of proteins, which is essential for the proper functioning of cellular processes and the overall physiology of an organism.

Table 2 List of the 64 possible codons used for protein synthesis

First Base in the Codon	Second base in the codon				Third Base in the Codon
	U	C	A	G	
U	UUU Phenylalanine	UCU Serine	UAU Tyrosine	UGU Cysteine	U
	UUC Phenylalanine	UCC Serine	UAC Tyrosine	UGC Cysteine	C
	UUA Leucine	UCA Serine	UAA * **STOP**	UGA* **STOP**	A
	UUG Leucine	UCG Serine	UAG * **STOP**	UGG Tryptophan	G
C	CUU Leucine	CCU Proline	CAU Histidine	CGU Arginine	U
	CUC Leucine	CCC Proline	CAC Histidine	CGC Arginine	C
	CUA Leucine	CCA Proline	CAA Glutamine	CGA Arginine	A
	CUG Leucine	CCG Proline	CAG Glutamine	CGG Arginine	G
A	AUU Isoleucine	ACU Threonine	AAU Asparagine	AGU Serine	U
	AUC Isoleucine	ACC Threonine	AAC Asparagine	AGC Serine	C
	AUA Isoleucine	ACA Threonine	AAA Lysine	AGA Arginine	A
	AUG Methionine	ACG Threonine	AAG Lysine	AGG Arginine	G
G	GUU Valine	GCU Alanine	GAU Aspartic Acid	GGU Glycine	U
	GUC Valine	GCC Alanine	GAC Aspartic Acid	GGC Glycine	C
	GUA Valine	GCA Alanine	GAA Glutamic Acid	GGA Glycine	A
	GUG Valine	GCG Alanine	GAG Glutamic Acid	GGG Glycine	G

4.1.1.5. Importance of Primary Structure:

The primary structure of a protein is fundamental to its overall biological function and higher-order structural organization. This sequence of amino acids forms the foundation for the secondary, tertiary, and quaternary structures of the protein, which ultimately determine its specific shape and functionality. The precise arrangement of amino acids is crucial, as even minor alterations, such as mutations or changes in the amino acid sequence, can significantly impact protein folding, stability, and activity. Such disruptions can lead to various proteinopathies—diseases and disorders caused by misfolded or dysfunctional proteins. Understanding the primary structure is therefore essential for comprehending how proteins achieve their functional forms and for developing therapeutic strategies to address related diseases.

4.1.2 Secondary Structure:

The secondary structure of a protein pertains to the local folding patterns and spatial arrangements of amino acid residues within the polypeptide chain, forming specific structural motifs. This level of organization is primarily characterized by two regular and repetitive conformations: alpha helices and beta sheets. Alpha helices are right-handed coils stabilized by hydrogen bonds between every fourth amino acid, creating a helical structure. In contrast, beta sheets consist of beta strands connected laterally by hydrogen bonds, forming sheet-like structures that can be parallel or antiparallel. These secondary structures play a crucial role in stabilizing the protein's overall architecture and influencing its higher-order folding and functionality. The formation and stability of these structures are essential for the protein's biological activity, as they contribute to the precise spatial arrangement necessary for interactions with other molecules and functional performance. Understanding secondary structure is key to deciphering protein function and designing therapeutic interventions for diseases caused by structural malformations.

4.1.2.1. Alpha Helix:

The alpha helix is a prevalent secondary structure motif in proteins, characterized by its right-handed helical shape. This structure is formed when the backbone of the polypeptide chain coils into a spiral, stabilized by intramolecular hydrogen bonds between the carbonyl oxygen of one amino acid and the amide hydrogen of another amino acid four residues ahead in the sequence. The alpha helix is tightly coiled, with 3.6 amino acid residues per turn, and each residue contributes a rise of 0.54 nm along the helical axis (Figure 4). The side chains of the amino acids extend outward from the helix, allowing them to interact with the surrounding environment. Alpha helices are particularly significant in proteins that span biological membranes, where their cylindrical shape makes them ideal for forming structural components or membrane-spanning domains. This configuration is crucial for the stability and function of membrane proteins, which are involved in various cellular processes such as signal transduction, transport, and cell adhesion. Understanding the formation and function of alpha helices provides insights into protein design and the development of therapeutic agents targeting helical regions in proteins.

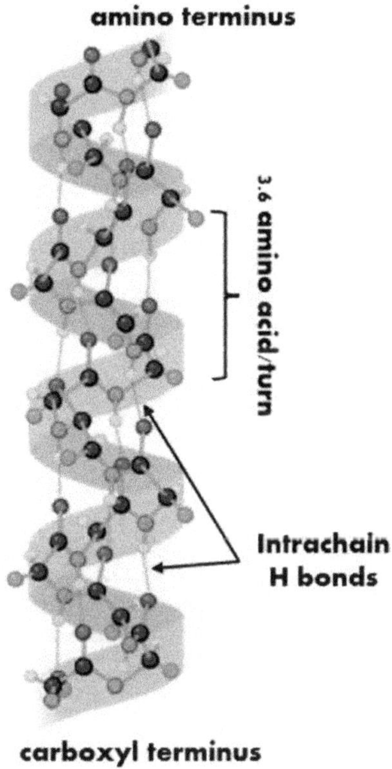

Figure 4 Structure of α helix

4.1.2.2. Beta (β) pleated Sheet:

A beta-pleated sheet is a common secondary structure motif in proteins, characterized by its planar, extended conformation. In this structure, adjacent segments of the polypeptide chain, known as beta strands, align side by side, allowing for the formation of hydrogen bonds between the backbone atoms of neighbouring strands. Beta sheets can be classified as either parallel or antiparallel, depending on the directionality of the strands relative to each other (Figure 5). In a parallel beta-sheet, the strands run in the same direction, whereas in an antiparallel beta-sheet, the strands run in opposite directions. Typically, beta strands consist of 3 to 10 amino acid residues, and their interaction through hydrogen bonding contributes significantly to the stability of the beta-sheet. These sheets play a crucial role in stabilizing the overall protein structure, often forming the core of the protein or serving as interfaces for protein-protein interactions. Beta sheets are also integral to the function of many proteins, particularly those involved in structural support, molecular recognition, and enzyme activity. Understanding beta sheets is essential for studying protein folding, stability, and the design of molecules that can interact with or disrupt these structures for therapeutic purposes.

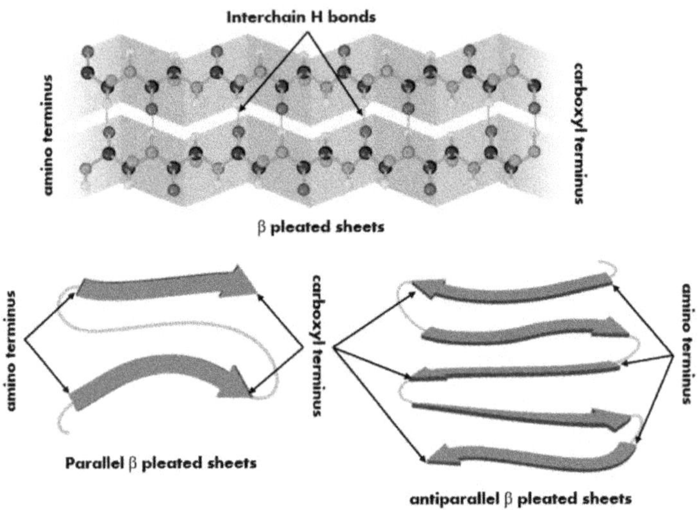

Figure 5 Structure and types of β-pleated Sheets

4.1.2.3. Other Secondary Structure Elements:

In addition to alpha helices and beta-pleated sheets, proteins often contain other secondary structure elements, such as beta turns and loops, which contribute to their overall architecture and function. Beta turns, also known as reverse or tight turns, are sharp directional changes in the polypeptide chain, typically involving four amino acid residues. These turns frequently occur on the protein surface and play a key role in protein folding and stability by allowing the chain to reverse direction. Loops, sometimes referred to as random coils, are regions of the polypeptide chain that do not adopt regular secondary structure patterns. These loops connect secondary structure elements and often form flexible regions that are crucial for protein-protein interactions, substrate binding, and dynamic movements within the protein. Together, these additional secondary structures complement the more rigid alpha helices and beta sheets, contributing to the intricate three-dimensional shape and functional versatility of proteins.

4.1.2.4. Importance of Secondary Structure:

The secondary structure of a protein is fundamental to its three-dimensional folding and biological function. It provides the stability, flexibility, and specificity required for the protein's overall structure, influencing essential processes such as protein-protein interactions, ligand binding, and enzymatic activity. The precise arrangement of secondary structures, such as alpha helices and beta sheets, is crucial for maintaining the integrity of the protein's architecture. Disruptions or alterations in these elements can have severe consequences, potentially leading to protein misfolding and associated diseases like Alzheimer's, Parkinson's, and amyotrophic lateral sclerosis (ALS). Understanding the role of secondary structure is therefore vital for exploring protein function and developing therapeutic strategies for related disorders.

4.1.3 Tertiary Structure:

The tertiary structure of a protein represents its overall three-dimensional conformation, arising from the folding and spatial arrangement of secondary structure elements like alpha helices and beta sheets into a compact, globular shape. This structure is stabilized by a variety of interactions between amino acid side chains, including hydrogen bonds, hydrophobic interactions, disulfide bridges, and electrostatic interactions. These interactions collectively determine the protein's stability and functionality, allowing it to perform specific biological tasks. The precise folding of the tertiary structure is critical, as even minor alterations can lead to misfolding, potentially causing diseases such as cystic fibrosis or certain types of cancer. Understanding the tertiary structure is essential for comprehending how proteins achieve their complex functions and for designing interventions that target specific protein conformations in therapeutic development.

4.1.3.1 Tertiary Structure Determinants:

The tertiary structure of a protein is fundamentally determined by its amino acid sequence, which directs the specific interactions and folding pathways required to achieve the native conformation. Protein folding occurs through a hierarchical process, beginning with the formation of secondary structure elements such as alpha helices and beta sheets. These elements then pack into the protein's final three-dimensional shape, guided by a combination of hydrophobic interactions, hydrogen bonding, and other stabilizing forces like disulfide bridges and electrostatic interactions. This intricate folding process ensures that the protein adopts its functional form, crucial for its biological activity. Disruptions in this folding pathway can lead to misfolding and associated diseases, underscoring the importance of understanding the mechanisms that drive protein tertiary structure formation for therapeutic and research applications.

4.1.3.2 Importance of Tertiary Structure:

The tertiary structure of a protein is crucial for its biological function, as it dictates the protein's activity, specificity, and interactions with other molecules. This three-dimensional conformation enables the precise positioning of active sites and binding interfaces essential for the protein's function. Any alterations in the tertiary structure, such as misfolding or unfolding, can disrupt these critical interactions and lead to a loss of function. Such structural changes are implicated in a range of diseases, including neurodegenerative disorders like Alzheimer's and Parkinson's, various cancers, and autoimmune diseases. Understanding the determinants and consequences of tertiary structure changes is vital for developing therapeutic strategies aimed at correcting or compensating for protein misfolding and dysfunction.

4.1.4 Quaternary Structure:

The quaternary structure of a protein refers to the arrangement and interactions between multiple polypeptide chains, or subunits, that come together to form a functional protein complex. Proteins exhibiting quaternary structure are composed of two or more polypeptide chains, each with its own tertiary structure. The assembly of these subunits into a quaternary structure is driven by a range of non-covalent interactions, including hydrogen bonds, hydrophobic interactions, electrostatic forces, and sometimes disulfide bonds. These interactions facilitate the proper alignment and functional integration of the subunits, enabling the protein complex to perform its biological roles effectively. Quaternary structure is crucial for the function of many proteins, such as hemoglobin, which relies on its tetrameric form to efficiently transport oxygen. Disruptions in quaternary structure can affect protein function and are implicated in various diseases, emphasizing the importance of understanding these complex protein assemblies for therapeutic and research purposes.

4.1.4.1. Multimeric Protein Complexes:

Proteins with quaternary structure are typically composed of two or more subunits, which can be either identical, known as oligomers, or non-identical, referred to as multimers. Each subunit contributes significantly to the overall structure and function of the protein complex. The interactions between these subunits, which include hydrogen bonds, hydrophobic interactions, electrostatic forces, and sometimes disulfide bonds, are crucial for stabilizing the quaternary structure. These interactions not only maintain the integrity of the protein complex but also enable it to perform its biological functions effectively. For instance, in hemoglobin, the quaternary structure allows for cooperative oxygen binding and release, essential for efficient oxygen transport in the blood. Understanding these interactions and the quaternary arrangement is fundamental for elucidating protein functionality and for designing targeted therapies that can modulate protein complexes in various diseases.

4.1.4.2. Assembly of Subunits:

The assembly of subunits into a quaternary structure is largely driven by complementary interactions between amino acid residues on different subunits. Non-covalent interactions, including hydrogen bonding, hydrophobic interactions, and electrostatic forces, play crucial roles in mediating the assembly and stabilizing the quaternary protein complexes. These interactions ensure that the subunits fit together correctly and maintain the integrity of the overall protein structure. In certain cases, disulfide bonds between cysteine residues on different subunits can also contribute additional stability to the quaternary structure, reinforcing the complex's robustness. Together, these forces enable the precise arrangement of subunits, which is essential for the protein's functional activity and structural integrity.

4.1.4.3. Symmetry and Arrangement:

Quaternary protein complexes often exhibit symmetry in the arrangement of their subunits, which can be rotational, translational, or helical. This symmetry can manifest as cyclic, where subunits are arranged in a circular or helical pattern, or dihedral, where they form planar or polyhedral arrangements. The specific arrangement of subunits within the quaternary structure is crucial for the protein complex's proper function, influencing processes such as substrate binding, catalysis, or allosteric regulation. Symmetry in quaternary structure facilitates efficient interaction between subunits and ensures that the protein complex can perform its biological roles with high precision and effectiveness.

4.1.4.4. Functional Significance:

The quaternary structure is crucial for the biological function of many proteins, especially those involved in complex biochemical processes or molecular recognition events. Protein complexes with quaternary structure often demonstrate enhanced functional properties, such as increased catalytic activity, greater substrate specificity, or refined regulatory control, compared to their individual subunits. The assembly of multiple subunits into a functional complex allows for sophisticated interactions and regulatory mechanisms that are vital for efficient biological function and adaptation.

4.1.4.5. Examples of Proteins with Quaternary Structure:

Many enzymes, receptors, transporters, and structural proteins exist as multimeric complexes with quaternary structure. For instance, hemoglobin comprises four globin subunits—two alpha and two beta chains—that assemble into a functional oxygen-binding protein, enabling efficient oxygen transport in the blood. Similarly, DNA polymerase is a multi-subunit enzyme involved in DNA replication, where its various subunits work together to ensure accurate and efficient synthesis of DNA. The quaternary structure of these proteins is essential for their functional properties, allowing them to perform complex biological tasks that individual subunits alone could not achieve.

4.1.4.6. Role in Protein Function and Regulation:

The quaternary structure of a protein complex plays a crucial role in influencing its stability, activity, and regulation. The specific arrangement and interactions of subunits within the complex can significantly impact its overall functionality. Changes in subunit composition or the assembly of these subunits can modulate the protein complex's activity, allowing for precise control of biological processes in response to cellular signals or environmental cues. This dynamic regulation enables proteins to adapt their functions as needed, ensuring that biological systems operate efficiently and effectively. For example, in hemoglobin, the binding of oxygen to one subunit enhances the binding affinity of the other subunits, demonstrating how quaternary structure can regulate protein function.

4.1.5 Interactions playing role in structure of protein

4.1.5.1. Hydrophobic Interactions:

Hydrophobic interactions are pivotal in protein folding and stability. Nonpolar (hydrophobic) amino acid side chains tend to cluster together in the protein's interior, away from the surrounding aqueous environment, to minimize their exposure to water molecules. This clustering of hydrophobic residues in the protein core leads to the formation of a hydrophobic core, which stabilizes the protein structure by reducing the free energy of the system. By minimizing contact between hydrophobic side chains and the aqueous environment, the protein achieves a more stable and energetically favourable conformation, essential for maintaining its functional integrity.

4.1.5.2. Hydrogen Bonding:

Hydrogen bonds are critical for the folding and stabilization of protein structures. These bonds form between polar or charged amino acid side chains and polar groups within the peptide backbone. Although hydrogen bonds are weaker than covalent bonds, they are abundant in proteins and provide directional interactions that are essential for defining secondary structure elements, such as alpha helices and beta sheets. Additionally, these bonds play a significant role in stabilizing the overall tertiary structure of proteins, ensuring that they maintain their functional three-dimensional conformation. Hydrogen bonds may be of two types i.e. intrachain or interchain hydrogen bonds as depicted in Figure 6.

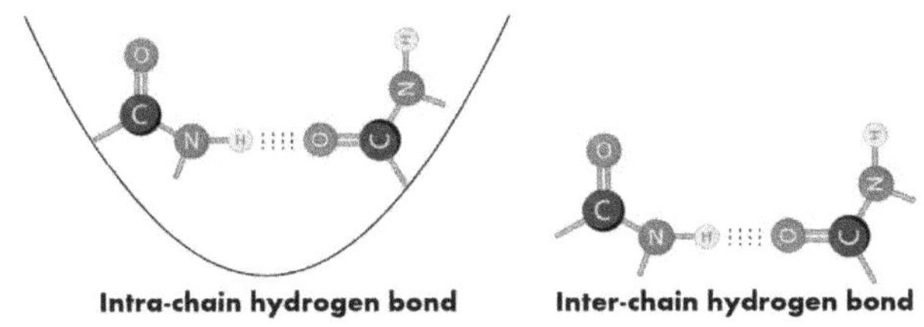

Figure 6 Types of hydrogen bonds found in proteins

4.1.5.3. Disulfide Bridges:

Disulfide bridges are covalent bonds formed between two cysteine residues through the oxidation of their sulfhydryl (-SH) groups, playing a crucial role in stabilizing protein structure (Figure 7). These bridges are particularly common in extracellular and secreted proteins, where they help maintain the tertiary structure and protect the protein from denaturation. By covalently linking distant regions of the polypeptide chain, disulfide bonds constrain the protein into its native conformation, providing additional stability against thermal and chemical denaturation. This ensures that the protein retains its functional three-dimensional structure under various environmental conditions.

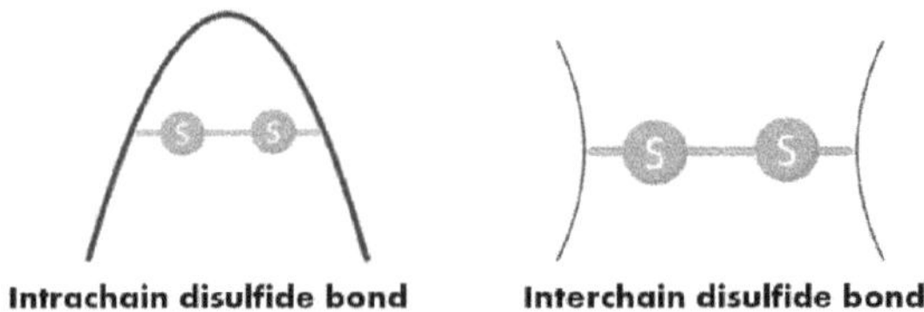

Figure 7 Types of disulphide bonds found in proteins

4.1.5.4. Electrostatic Interactions:

Electrostatic interactions, such as salt bridges and ion pairs, play a significant role in stabilizing protein structures by forming attractive forces between charged amino acid side chains. Positively charged side chains like those of lysine and arginine can form salt bridges with negatively charged side chains, such as those of aspartate and glutamate. These interactions not only stabilize the overall protein structure but also contribute to the stabilization of protein-protein interfaces and ligand binding sites, ensuring proper function and structural integrity in various biological processes.

CHAPTER V

Mechanism of Enzyme Action

The mechanism of enzyme action is a fundamental concept in biochemistry, explaining how enzymes catalyse biochemical reactions with remarkable specificity and efficiency. Recent advances in structural biology, computational modelling, and single-molecule techniques have provided deeper insights into enzyme dynamics, active site architecture, and the transition states of enzymatic reactions. Enzymes function by lowering the activation energy of a reaction, often through precise interactions within the active site, where substrates are oriented optimally for the reaction to proceed. New research highlights the importance of enzyme conformational changes, induced fit models, and the role of quantum mechanical effects in catalysis. These findings not only enhance our understanding of enzyme function but also pave the way for the development of novel biocatalysts and therapeutic agents through enzyme engineering and design.

5.1 Basic Mechanisms of Enzyme Action

5.1.1 Lowering Activation Energy

Enzymes lower the activation energy required for chemical reactions by stabilizing the transition state, thereby enabling reactions to occur more rapidly. Activation energy is the energy barrier that reactants must overcome to transform into products. By binding to their substrates, enzymes create a more favourable environment for the transition state, reducing the energy needed to reach it. This stabilization occurs through various mechanisms, such as precise substrate orientation, strain induction, covalent catalysis, or electrostatic interactions. Importantly, while enzymes accelerate the reaction rate, they do not alter the reaction's equilibrium position; they simply allow equilibrium to be reached more quickly by lowering the energy required to cross the activation energy barrier.

The effect of enzymes on the activation energy of a chemical reaction is shown in Figure 1. The upper curve represents the energy profile of a reaction without an enzyme, where a significant amount of energy, known as the activation energy, is required to reach the transition state. The lower curve demonstrates how the presence of an enzyme lowers this activation energy, allowing the reaction to occur more efficiently. Although the enzyme reduces the energy barrier, the total energy released during the reaction remains the same, as indicated by the energy difference between reactants and products. This highlights the enzyme's role as a catalyst: accelerating the reaction by lowering the activation energy, without altering the overall free energy change or equilibrium position of the reaction.

Activation Energy of Enzyme

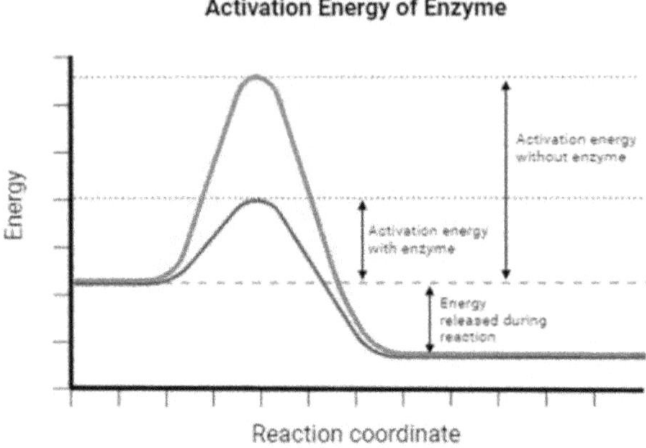

Figure 1 Effect of enzymes on the activation energy of a chemical reaction

5.2 Substrate Binding and Formation of the Enzyme-Substrate Complex

The initial step in enzyme action involves substrate binding to the enzyme's active site, forming the enzyme-substrate complex (ES). This interaction is often modelled by the "lock and key" or "induced fit" theories:

- **Lock and Key Model:** Proposed by **Emil Fischer** in 1894, this model suggests that the enzyme's active site has a specific geometric shape that fits only a particular substrate, much like a key fits a lock. However, this theory does not account for the flexibility of enzymes.
- **Induced Fit Model:** Developed by **Daniel Koshland** in 1958, this model posits that enzyme active sites are flexible, and upon substrate binding, the enzyme undergoes a conformational change that facilitates a more precise fit. This model better explains the dynamics of enzyme-substrate interactions, particularly the flexibility of the active site and the role of allosteric regulation.

5.3 Formation of the Transition State

The **transition state** is a high-energy, unstable intermediate that the substrate must pass through for the reaction to occur. It represents the point at which old bonds are breaking, and new bonds are forming, and is the most difficult phase of the reaction to achieve. The formation and stabilization of this transition state is the critical role of enzymes in lowering the **activation energy** required for the reaction. Enzymes do not alter the overall free energy change of the reaction but rather facilitate reaching the transition state more quickly and with less energy input. By precisely positioning the substrate within the active site and forming favourable interactions with the transition state, enzymes dramatically enhance the reaction rate. This process of **transition state stabilization** is the cornerstone of enzyme catalysis, achieved through several mechanisms:

5.3.1 Electrostatic Interactions Between Charged Amino Acids and Substrate

Enzymes often use **electrostatic interactions** to stabilize the transition state by forming **ionic bonds** with the substrate. These interactions occur between charged amino acid residues in the enzyme's active site and the oppositely charged regions of the substrate or its transition state. For example, positively charged amino acids such as **arginine** or **lysine** may interact with negatively charged substrate groups like phosphate ions or carboxylate groups. These electrostatic forces help to stabilize the transition state by lowering the energy required to form the intermediate, particularly in reactions where charge separation or charge redistribution occurs. In some cases, enzymes may even expel water molecules from the active site, creating a **hydrophobic environment** that further enhances electrostatic interactions. By precisely aligning these charged interactions, enzymes can significantly lower the activation energy and facilitate the transition to the product.

5.3.2 Hydrogen Bonding to Stabilize the Substrate's Intermediate Forms

Hydrogen bonds are another key stabilizing force used by enzymes to support the substrate as it passes through its transition state. These bonds form when hydrogen atoms, typically from polar groups on the substrate, interact with electronegative atoms like oxygen or nitrogen in the enzyme's active site. The transient hydrogen bonds stabilize the high-energy intermediate by anchoring the substrate and preventing it from reverting to its original form. Hydrogen bonding helps position the substrate correctly for the reaction and reduces the energy barrier for reaching the transition state. The enzyme may offer multiple hydrogen-bonding sites to ensure the stability of various intermediate forms during the reaction. These interactions are particularly important in **polar reactions** where the formation or rearrangement of polar groups is crucial to the mechanism. By maintaining substrate orientation and stabilizing the intermediate, hydrogen bonds play a significant role in ensuring efficient catalysis.

5.3.3 Covalent Catalysis: Formation of Temporary Covalent Bonds with the Substrate

In **covalent catalysis**, the enzyme forms **temporary covalent bonds** with the substrate during the reaction, creating a short-lived enzyme-substrate intermediate. This mechanism involves the active participation of amino acid residues in the enzyme that possess nucleophilic (electron-donating) properties, such as **serine, cysteine,** or **histidine**. These residues can attack the substrate's electrophilic (electron-deficient) centres, forming a covalent bond that alters the substrate's electronic structure, thus lowering the activation energy required to achieve the transition state. The enzyme, in this case, becomes an active participant in the chemical reaction, with the covalent bond formation leading to a stable intermediate. Once the transition state is reached and the reaction proceeds, the covalent bond is broken, and the enzyme returns to its original state. Covalent catalysis is commonly observed in **proteolytic enzymes** like **chymotrypsin** and **serine proteases**, where a serine residue in the active site temporarily forms a covalent bond with the substrate to facilitate peptide bond cleavage.

Through these mechanisms—**electrostatic interactions, hydrogen bonding,** and **covalent catalysis**—enzymes effectively stabilize the transition state of a reaction, significantly lowering the activation energy and facilitating rapid catalysis. Each interaction helps align the substrate properly, reduce the energy barrier, and guide the substrate through its high-energy intermediate form toward the formation of the product. This transition state stabilization is essential for the remarkable catalytic power of enzymes, enabling them to accelerate biological reactions by factors of millions or even billions.

5.4 Catalytic Mechanisms Employed by Enzymes

Enzymes, as biological catalysts, accelerate chemical reactions by employing a variety of catalytic mechanisms that lower the activation energy and facilitate the conversion of substrates into products. These mechanisms are highly specialized, depending on the nature of the reaction and the specific enzyme involved. Enzymes achieve their catalytic efficiency by utilizing strategies such as **acid-base catalysis**, where proton transfer aids the reaction; **covalent catalysis**, where transient enzyme-substrate bonds form; and **metal ion catalysis**, where metal ions stabilize reaction intermediates. Additionally, enzymes optimize reactions through **proximity and orientation effects**, bringing substrates into close alignment, and by imposing **strain or distortion** on substrates, mimicking the high-energy transition state. Each of these mechanisms is crucial for the precise and efficient control of biochemical processes in living organisms, making enzymes essential for life.

5.4.1 Acid-Base Catalysis

Acid-base catalysis is a fundamental mechanism used by many enzymes to accelerate biochemical reactions. In this process, amino acid residues within the enzyme's active site either donate protons (act as acids) or accept protons (act as bases) to stabilize reaction intermediates, thereby facilitating the reaction. This proton transfer is critical in lowering the activation energy of the reaction, particularly in reactions involving protonation or deprotonation of substrates.

Many enzymes employ **histidine** residues in acid-base catalysis due to histidine's unique pKa, which is near physiological pH. This makes histidine well-suited to function as both a proton donor and acceptor depending on the local environment of the enzyme active site. **Glutamic acid, aspartic acid**, and **lysine** can also serve as acid or base catalysts, depending on the type of reaction.

* **Example:** In the protease **chymotrypsin, histidine-57** plays a crucial role as a base catalyst. It abstracts a proton from **serine-195**, converting the serine residue into a potent nucleophile. This allows serine-195 to attack the carbonyl group of the substrate's peptide bond, initiating a series of events that ultimately cleave the peptide bond. After the reaction, histidine donates a proton to complete the catalytic cycle, demonstrating how enzymes can both donate and accept protons to facilitate reactions.

5.4.2 Covalent Catalysis

In **covalent catalysis**, the enzyme forms a temporary covalent bond with the substrate, resulting in an intermediate that often leads to a lower-energy reaction pathway. This mechanism involves nucleophilic amino acid residues in the enzyme, such as **serine, cysteine, lysine**, or **histidine**, which attack electrophilic centres on the substrate. The formation of this transient enzyme-substrate covalent complex facilitates the transformation of the substrate into the product, often by stabilizing reaction intermediates or by providing a new pathway for the reaction that requires less activation energy.

- **Example: Serine proteases** such as **trypsin** and **chymotrypsin** are classic examples of enzymes that use covalent catalysis. In these enzymes, the **serine residue** in the active site forms a covalent bond with the substrate's carbonyl carbon during peptide bond cleavage. The serine residue acts as a nucleophile, attacking the substrate and forming a **tetrahedral intermediate**, which subsequently breaks down to release the cleaved peptide. This mechanism lowers the energy required for bond breakage and allows the enzyme to catalyse the reaction efficiently.

5.4.3 Metal Ion Catalysis

Metal ion catalysis is a common catalytic strategy used by enzymes that involve **transition metals** like **zinc (Zn^{2+})**, **magnesium (Mg^{2+})**, iron **(Fe^{2+}/Fe^{3+})**, or **manganese (Mn^{2+})**. These metal ions participate directly in the catalytic process by stabilizing negative charges on intermediates, serving as electrophiles that attract electron-rich groups, or by facilitating **redox reactions** (oxidation-reduction processes).

Metal ions often play a crucial role in **polarizing water molecules** or other substrates, making them more reactive. For instance, metal ions can make a water molecule more nucleophilic, enhancing its ability to attack electrophilic centres on substrates.

- **Example:** In **carbonic anhydrase**, a zinc ion (Zn^{2+}) is critical for catalysis. The zinc ion coordinates with a water molecule, increasing its nucleophilicity by promoting the release of a proton. This activation of water enables it to attack carbon dioxide (CO_2), facilitating the conversion of CO_2 into bicarbonate (HCO_3^-). This reaction is essential for maintaining acid-base balance in the blood and tissues. The zinc ion plays a direct role in the catalytic process by stabilizing the transition state and lowering the activation energy required for the reaction.

5.4.4 Proximity and Orientation Effects

Enzymes achieve remarkable catalytic efficiency by bringing reactants into close **proximity** and orienting them correctly for the reaction. This mechanism, known as **proximity and orientation effects**, enhances reaction rates by reducing the entropic cost of bringing two reacting molecules together in solution. In solution, molecules move randomly, and without the guidance of an enzyme, substrates may collide with each other in a non-optimal orientation, resulting in a low probability of reaction.

Enzymes overcome this limitation by binding substrates at specific orientations and distances that favour the formation of the transition state. This not only increases the likelihood of productive collisions between reacting species but also ensures that reactive groups are aligned correctly to participate in the reaction.

- **Example**: In **DNA polymerase**, the enzyme responsible for synthesizing new DNA strands, the enzyme carefully positions the nucleotide substrates in close proximity to the growing DNA chain. The correct orientation of the incoming nucleotides ensures that the **3'-OH group** of the growing DNA strand can effectively attack the **5'-phosphate group** of the incoming nucleotide, enabling the formation of a phosphodiester bond. By ensuring precise alignment, DNA polymerase dramatically accelerates the rate of DNA synthesis.

5.4.5 Strain and Distortion

Enzymes can also catalyse reactions by imposing **strain or distortion** on the substrate, forcing it into a conformation that resembles the **transition state**. This strategy reduces the energy barrier required to achieve the transition state by destabilizing the ground state of the substrate. Enzymes may achieve this by binding the substrate in a strained or distorted conformation, mimicking the high-energy transition state that the substrate must pass through.

This strain or distortion helps weaken the bonds that need to be broken and facilitates the rearrangement of atoms required for the reaction to occur. By doing so, the enzyme effectively lowers the activation energy and speeds up the conversion of substrate to product.

- **Example**: In the enzyme **lysozyme**, which catalyses the cleavage of **peptidoglycan** in bacterial cell walls, the enzyme binds the substrate in such a way that it distorts the bond between sugars in the peptidoglycan chain. This distortion mimics the transition state, making it easier for the enzyme to catalyse the hydrolysis of the glycosidic bond. The induced strain facilitates the breakdown of bacterial cell walls, making lysozyme a powerful antibacterial agent.

Through these diverse catalytic mechanisms—**acid-base catalysis, covalent catalysis, metal ion catalysis, proximity and orientation effects,** and **strain or distortion**—enzymes efficiently lower the activation energy of biochemical reactions. Each of these strategies is fine-tuned to the specific nature of the enzyme and its substrate, allowing enzymes to catalyse reactions with extraordinary speed and specificity, essential for the proper functioning of biological systems.

CHAPTER VI

Lock and Key Model

The **Lock and Key Model** of enzyme action, proposed by German chemist **Emil Fischer in 1894**, was one of the earliest theories developed to explain the specificity of enzyme-substrate interactions. This model likened the enzyme-substrate relationship to a lock and key, where the enzyme (the "lock") has a specific and rigid structure that fits only one type of substrate (the "key"). According to this model, the enzyme's active site, which is the region of the enzyme where the substrate binds and the reaction takes place, is a rigid structure pre-formed in such a way that it only accommodates a particular substrate, just as a key fit into its corresponding lock.

6.1 Enzyme-Substrate Complex Formation as per Lock and Key Model:

The mechanism of enzyme-substrate complex formation involves several key steps, each crucial for the efficient catalysis of biochemical reactions. Here's a detailed explanation of the process:

6.1.1. Recognition:

The initial step in enzyme-substrate complex formation involves the recognition of the substrate by the enzyme's active site. This process begins with the substrate approaching the enzyme and binding to its active site through a range of non-covalent interactions. These include hydrogen bonding, van der Waals forces, and hydrophobic interactions, all of which facilitate the substrate's attachment to the enzyme. The active site of the enzyme is specifically designed with structural features that complement the chemical structure of the substrate. This complementary arrangement allows for selective recognition and precise binding, ensuring that only substrates with the appropriate shape and chemical properties can interact effectively with the enzyme. This specificity is crucial for the enzyme's catalytic activity and overall function, enabling it to perform its role efficiently within biochemical pathways.

6.1.2. Formation of Enzyme-Substrate Complex:

Once the substrate binds to the enzyme's active site, the enzyme undergoes conformational changes to better accommodate the substrate molecule. This phenomenon, known as induced fit, involves alterations in the shape and flexibility of the active site to optimize interactions between the enzyme and the substrate. The enzyme's active site adjusts to the substrate's shape, ensuring a more precise fit and enhancing the enzyme's catalytic efficiency. As a result of this conformational change, the reactive groups of the substrate are brought into close proximity with the catalytic residues within the active site. This positioning is crucial for facilitating the subsequent chemical reactions, as it aligns the substrate in a manner that promotes the formation of the transition state and accelerates the conversion of the substrate into a product.

6.1.3. Catalysis:

Within the enzyme-substrate complex, the enzyme plays a crucial role in facilitating the conversion of the substrate into products by lowering the activation energy barrier required for the reaction to proceed. The enzyme achieves this by stabilizing the transition state, a high-energy intermediate that forms during the transformation of the substrate into the product. This stabilization is accomplished through several mechanisms: the enzyme aligns reactive groups in the substrate, provides catalytic residues that directly participate in the chemical reaction, and modifies the local chemical environment within the active site to favour the reaction. By reducing the activation energy barrier, enzymes effectively increase the reaction rate, enabling the reaction to proceed more rapidly and efficiently under physiological conditions. This ability to accelerate reactions is fundamental to maintaining the dynamic and regulated processes of life.

6.1.4. Release of Products:

After the catalytic reaction has occurred, the products of the reaction are released from the enzyme's active site. This release is often facilitated by further conformational changes in the enzyme, which may revert to its original state or adjust to accommodate the new position of the substrate or products. These changes help to free the products from the active site, ensuring that the enzyme is available for subsequent catalytic cycles. The completion of the product release marks the end of one catalytic cycle, allowing the enzyme to continue its role as a catalyst in various cellular processes. This continuous cycle of substrate binding, catalysis, and product release is essential for maintaining the efficiency and regulation of biochemical pathways within the cell.

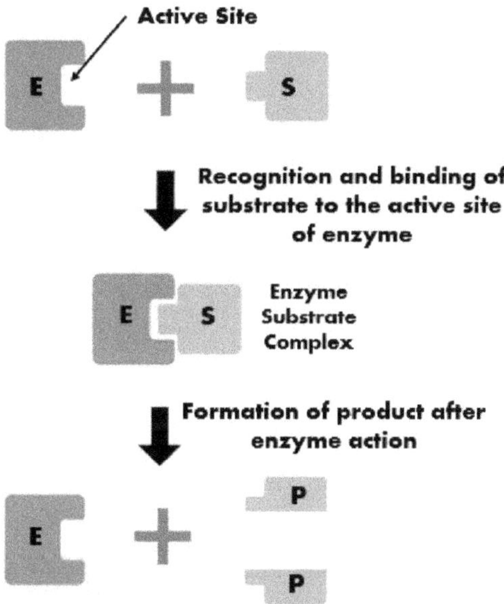

Figure 1Lock and Key Model: Mechanism of action of Enzymes on substrate leads to the formation of products. (**E: Enzyme, S: Substrate, P: Product)**

6.2 Merits of the Lock and Key Model

The **Lock and Key Model** emphasizes the **specificity** of enzymes and helps to explain why enzymes are capable of catalysing only certain reactions. This specificity is crucial for maintaining the efficiency and order of biochemical processes in living organisms. For instance, the enzyme sucrase will only bind to sucrose and catalyse its breakdown into glucose and fructose, while other sugars, such as lactose or maltose, will not fit into sucrase's active site.

Furthermore, this model helps illustrate the importance of **enzyme-substrate interactions** in maintaining metabolic control within cells. The highly specific nature of enzyme binding ensures that only the intended reactions occur, preventing unwanted side reactions that could be detrimental to the organism.

6.3 Limitations of the Lock and Key Model

While the **Lock and Key Model** is useful in explaining enzyme specificity, it has several limitations and does not account for all the behaviours observed in enzymatic reactions. The most significant limitation is the model's assumption that enzymes and their active sites are rigid, inflexible structures.

6.3.1 Lack of Enzyme Flexibility: The **Lock and Key Model** assumes that the active site of the enzyme is pre-formed in a rigid shape, complementary to the substrate. However, advances in structural biology have shown that enzymes are not rigid but rather dynamic molecules. Many enzymes exhibit flexibility, allowing their active sites to adjust and mold around the substrate upon binding. This phenomenon, where the enzyme changes shape to accommodate the substrate, is better explained by the **Induced Fit Model**, introduced by Daniel Koshland in 1958.

6.3.2 Excludes Induced Fit and Transition State Stabilization: The Lock and Key Model does not account for the fact that enzymes often undergo subtle conformational changes that further stabilize the transition state of the substrate. These changes help to reduce the activation energy of the reaction and make the catalytic process more efficient. The **Induced Fit Model** addresses this limitation by incorporating enzyme flexibility and transition state stabilization into the explanation of enzyme action.

6.3.3 Inability to Explain Non-Specific Interactions: Some enzymes exhibit a degree of **promiscuity**, meaning they can bind to multiple substrates or catalyse reactions with different molecules, especially when the substrates are structurally similar. The Lock and Key Model, with its rigid specificity, cannot explain these cases. In contrast, the Induced Fit Model can accommodate the flexibility required for enzymes to interact with a broader range of substrates.

6.3.4 Fails to Address Regulatory Mechanisms: Enzymes are subject to various regulatory mechanisms, such as allosteric modulation, where the binding of a molecule at a site other than the active site changes the enzyme's shape and activity. The Lock and Key Model, which portrays enzymes as rigid entities, does not easily explain these dynamic regulatory effects, further highlighting its limitations in the context of modern enzymology.

CHAPTER VII

Induced Fit Model

The **Induced Fit Model**, developed by **Daniel Koshland in 1958**, revolutionized the understanding of enzyme-substrate interactions by introducing the concept of enzyme flexibility. Unlike the earlier **Lock and Key Model**, which suggested that enzymes have rigid active sites that perfectly match the substrate, the Induced Fit Model posits that the active site of the enzyme is flexible and changes shape when the substrate binds. This dynamic model provides a more accurate representation of how enzymes function, particularly in light of their ability to interact with a broader range of substrates and engage in regulatory mechanisms such as allosteric modulation.

7.1 Concepts of the Induced Fit Model

7.1.1 Active Site Flexibility: The most significant innovation of the Induced Fit Model is the idea that an enzyme's active site is not pre-formed in a perfect shape to bind the substrate. Instead, the enzyme undergoes a **conformational change** when the substrate approaches, moulding itself around the substrate to create a more precise and complementary fit. This flexibility enhances the enzyme's catalytic efficiency by optimizing the positioning of key residues involved in the chemical reaction.

7.1.2 Substrate-Induced Conformational Change: When a substrate binds to the enzyme, it induces a **structural rearrangement** in the enzyme. This change can involve both the active site and other regions of the enzyme, allowing the enzyme to better accommodate the substrate. This induced fit creates an environment that stabilizes the transition state of the substrate, thereby lowering the activation energy required for the reaction and making the reaction proceed more quickly.

7.1.3 Transition State Stabilization: The conformational change that occurs in the Induced Fit Model allows the enzyme to stabilize the **transition state** of the substrate more effectively than if the enzyme remained rigid. By facilitating this transition state, the enzyme lowers the activation energy required for the reaction, allowing it to proceed at a much faster rate. This transition state stabilization is a key feature of the Induced Fit Model and helps explain why enzymes are such powerful catalysts.

7.1.4 Allosteric Regulation: The Induced Fit Model also helps explain the phenomenon of **allosteric regulation**, where molecules binding at sites other than the active site (allosteric sites) cause conformational changes that alter the enzyme's activity. These conformational shifts can either enhance or inhibit the enzyme's ability to catalyze its specific reaction. In the context of the Induced Fit Model, such regulatory molecules may influence the enzyme's shape, modulating how well it can bind to its substrate and catalyze the reaction.

7.1.5 Broad Substrate Specificity: While the Lock and Key Model emphasized the rigid specificity of enzymes for their substrates, the Induced Fit Model allows for **greater versatility**. Because the active site is flexible, enzymes can accommodate a range of substrates that share structural similarities. This explains why certain enzymes can catalyze reactions involving more than one type of substrate, or why they can catalyze different types of reactions depending on environmental factors or regulatory mechanisms.

7.2 Mechanism of the Induced Fit Model

The detailed procedure of this mechanism is explained below and represented in the accompanying Figure 1.

7.2.1. Initial Binding

In the first stage of the Induced Fit Model, the substrate approaches the enzyme's active site. Unlike the rigid **Lock and Key Model**, where the active site is already perfectly shaped to accommodate the substrate, the **Induced Fit Model** suggests that the active site may not be fully formed at this point. Instead, the enzyme is somewhat flexible, with the active site in a state that only partially matches the substrate. As the substrate draws near, weak, non-covalent interactions, such as **hydrogen bonds**, **ionic interactions**, or **hydrophobic forces**, help the substrate align with the enzyme's active site. These interactions are sufficient to hold the substrate in proximity but do not yet represent the final conformation needed for catalysis. This initial loose interaction triggers the next stage—inducing a change in the enzyme's structure.

7.2.2. Induced Conformational Change

Once the substrate is bound loosely to the enzyme's active site, more specific and intimate interactions begin to form. The binding of the substrate induces a **conformational change** in the enzyme—a pivotal aspect of the **Induced Fit Model**. This means that the enzyme's structure, particularly its active site, changes shape to more precisely accommodate the substrate. The interactions between the substrate and certain **amino acid residues** of the enzyme play a key role in this process. The enzyme essentially "molds" itself around the substrate, ensuring a much closer and more precise fit. This conformational adjustment allows the enzyme to better stabilize the substrate's **transition state**, which is the highly reactive and unstable intermediate form that must be achieved during the reaction. This stage is crucial because it allows the enzyme to align critical amino acid residues properly, positioning them for catalysis.

7.2.3. Catalysis

With the enzyme's active site now fully conformed to fit the substrate, the reaction is ready to proceed. During this phase, the enzyme catalyses the conversion of the substrate into its product(s). The precise positioning of the substrate within the enzyme's active site allows for the optimal interaction of catalytic residues with the substrate, facilitating the chemical reaction. The enzyme's role is to stabilize the **transition state**, an unstable intermediate stage that the substrate must pass through to convert into the product. By stabilizing this state, the enzyme significantly lowers the **activation energy** required for the reaction, making the process more efficient. The enzyme may also provide an environment that favours the formation of the product, such as by providing or removing protons (acid/ base catalysis), positioning substrates for covalent bond formation (covalent catalysis), or promoting the correct orientation for the reaction to occur.

7.2.4. Product Release

After the catalytic reaction has taken place, the substrate is transformed into the product(s). At this stage, the enzyme undergoes another conformational shift, releasing the product from the active site. The product no longer fits perfectly within the active site, and its altered shape or properties result in its weaker binding to the enzyme. The products are then released, and the enzyme reverts to its original form, ready to catalyse another round of reactions. This restoration of the enzyme's original conformation is important for its ability to be reused multiple times, as enzymes act as **biological catalysts** that are not consumed in the reaction. The enzyme can now bind to a new substrate molecule, repeating the process. This cyclical nature of enzyme catalysis underscores its efficiency and role in biological systems.

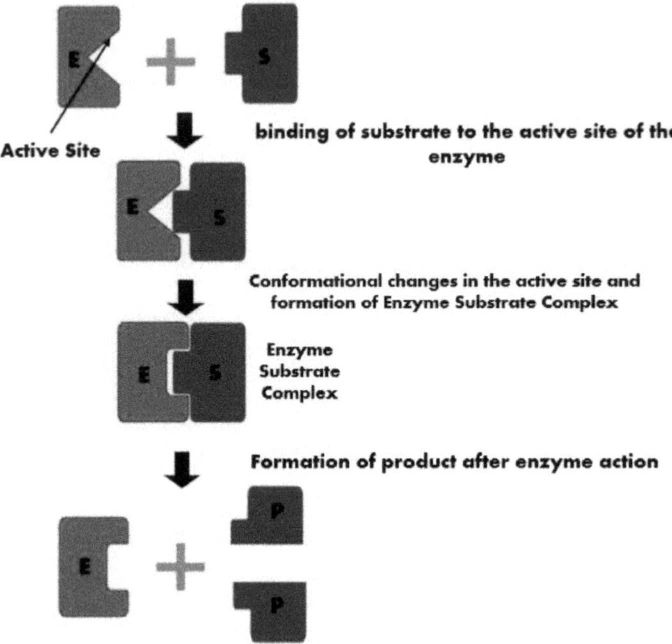

Figure 1 Induced Fit Model: Mechanism of action of Enzymes on substrate leads to the formation of products by conformational changes in the active site of the enzyme. (**E: Enzyme, S: Substrate, P: Product**)

7.3 Advantages of the Induced Fit Model

7.3.1 More Accurate Representation of Enzyme Dynamics: The **Induced Fit Model** provides a better explanation for the dynamic nature of enzymes compared to the rigid Lock and Key Model. By accounting for conformational changes, this model aligns with modern structural biology data that show enzymes are flexible molecules, capable of shifting their shapes during the course of substrate binding and catalysis.

7.3.2 Explanation of Broad Substrate Specificity: Some enzymes exhibit **substrate promiscuity**, meaning they can catalyse reactions with multiple substrates, or different reactions with the same substrate. The flexibility of the enzyme's active site in the Induced Fit Model allows for a broader range of interactions than the Lock and Key Model, making it a more versatile and realistic explanation of enzyme activity.

7.3.3 Allosteric Regulation: The Induced Fit Model also offers a framework for understanding **allosteric regulation**, where binding of molecules at sites other than the active site leads to conformational changes that affect enzyme activity. This ability to regulate enzymatic activity is crucial in many biological pathways where enzymes must be turned on or off depending on the cell's needs.

7.3.4 Support from Structural Biology: The **Induced Fit Model** is supported by modern techniques such as X-ray crystallography and nuclear magnetic resonance (NMR), which have revealed that many enzymes do indeed undergo conformational changes upon substrate binding. These structural insights affirm the concept that enzymes are not static entities but dynamic molecules that adapt to their substrates.

7.4 Limitations of the Induced Fit Model

While the **Induced Fit Model** has been highly successful in explaining the behaviour of most enzymes, there are still some limitations:

7.4.1 Not Universal: Although many enzymes fit the Induced Fit Model, some enzyme-substrate interactions seem to align more closely with the **Lock and Key Model**. For certain enzymes, the active site does appear to be pre-formed to match the substrate, without significant conformational changes.

7.4.2 Does Not Fully Explain Transition State Stabilization: While the Induced Fit Model introduces the idea of conformational change to stabilize the transition state, it does not always provide a detailed mechanism for how this stabilization occurs. Other models and refinements, such as the **transition state theory**, might be necessary to complement this model for specific enzyme systems.

7.4.3 Complexity in Allosteric Modulation: Although the Induced Fit Model accounts for allosteric regulation, this area remains highly complex, and additional models, such as **cooperative binding models** for multimeric enzymes, are needed to fully explain how allosteric regulation impacts enzymatic activity.

CHAPTER VIII

Enzyme Kinetics: Michaelis–Menten Equation

Enzyme kinetics is a critical field of study within biochemistry that focuses on the rates at which enzymatic reactions occur, providing essential insights into the mechanisms by which enzymes catalyse biological processes. Understanding the principles of enzyme kinetics is foundational for exploring metabolic pathways, drug design, and biotechnology applications. Key concepts such as Michaelis-Menten kinetics, enzyme inhibition, and allosteric regulation form the basis of this analysis. Recent research highlights novel methods for quantifying enzyme activity in complex biological systems, such as the development of single-molecule techniques and advanced computational models, which allow for a more precise understanding of enzyme behaviour under physiological conditions. These advancements underscore the importance of enzyme kinetics in addressing current challenges in medicine and industrial biotechnology.

8.1 Michaelis-Menten Equation:

The Michaelis-Menten equation is a foundational mathematical model in enzymology that describes the kinetics of enzyme-catalyzed reactions. Developed by **Leonor Michaelis** and **Maud Menten** in 1913, it provides a quantitative relationship between the reaction velocity (v) and the substrate concentration ([S]) under specific assumptions, such as the formation of an enzyme-substrate complex and the steady-state condition (Figure 1). The Michaelis-Menten equation is typically expressed as follows:

$$V = \frac{V_{max}\ [S]}{K_m + [S]}$$

where,

v = initial reaction velocity, or the rate of the formation of product per unit time

V_{max} = maximum reaction velocity, representing the rate of the reaction when all enzyme's active sites are saturated with substrate

[S] = Substrate concentration

K_m = Michaelis constant, which is a measure of the enzyme's affinity for its substrate. It is defined as the substrate concentration at which the reaction rate is half of V_{max}

This model remains a cornerstone in enzymology, enabling researchers to understand catalytic efficiency and enzyme behaviour in different environments. Recent advancements in enzyme kinetics, including the use of computational models and single-molecule techniques, have refined our understanding of the Michaelis-Menten equation, making it applicable to complex, multi-enzyme systems and non-ideal conditions in modern research.

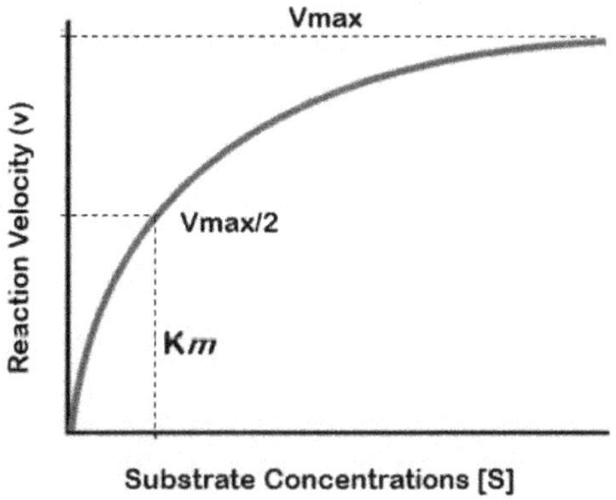

Figure 1 This plot shows the expected reaction velocity from the Michaelis-Menten equation as a function of substrate concentration and illustrates the importance of the kinetic parameters V_{max} and K_m.

8.2 Assumptions of the Michaelis-Menten Equation:

The Michaelis-Menten equation is based on several key assumptions that simplify the analysis of enzyme-catalysed reactions. First, it assumes that the formation of the enzyme-substrate complex (ES) is the rate-limiting step of the reaction, meaning that the conversion of the ES complex to product is slower than the binding of the substrate to the enzyme. Second, the steady-state assumption posits that the concentration of the ES complex remains relatively constant throughout the reaction, as the rate of its formation is balanced by the rate of its breakdown into either the free enzyme and substrate or the enzyme and product. Finally, the model assumes that the total enzyme concentration remains constant, with only a small fraction of the enzyme bound to the substrate at any given time. These assumptions allow the derivation of a simplified kinetic equation that is applicable under ideal conditions, making it a widely used tool in enzymology for analysing reaction rates and enzyme efficiency.

8.3 Interpretation of the Michaelis-Menten Equation:

At low substrate concentrations ($[S]<<Km$), the Michaelis-Menten equation simplifies to.

$$V = \frac{V_{max}\,[S]}{K_m}$$

In this regime, the rate of the reaction is directly proportional to the substrate concentration, following first-order kinetics. At high substrate concentrations ($[S]>>K_m$), the term $[S]$ dominates the denominator of the equation, and the rate of the reaction approaches V_{max}, becoming independent of substrate concentration and following zero-order kinetics.

$$V = V_{max}$$

The Michaelis constant K_m provides a measure of the enzyme's affinity for its substrate. Enzymes with lower K_m values have higher substrate affinity, while enzymes with higher K_m values have lower substrate affinity. The ratio V_{max}/K_m is often used as a kinetic parameter to characterize enzyme-substrate interactions and compare the catalytic efficiencies of different enzymes.

8.4 Enzyme Kinetic Parameters:

8.4.1 Michaelis Constant (K_m):

The Michaelis constant (K_m) is a crucial parameter in enzyme kinetics that quantifies the affinity of an enzyme for its substrate. It is defined as the substrate concentration at which the reaction rate is half of the maximum reaction velocity (V_{max}). The Michaelis constant is named after **Leonor Michaelis**, one of the scientists who developed the Michaelis-Menten equation, which describes enzyme kinetics.

At

$$V = \frac{V_{max}}{2}$$

Mathematically, the Michaelis constant is represented as:

$$K_m = [S]$$

Where,

K_m = Michaelis constant

V_{max} = maximum reaction velocity

[S] = substrate concentration

8.4.2 Interpretation of the Michaelis Constant:

A lower K_m value indicates higher substrate affinity, meaning the enzyme can achieve half of its maximum reaction velocity at lower substrate concentrations. Enzymes with low K_m values are more efficient at binding substrates. A higher K_m value indicates lower substrate affinity, meaning the enzyme requires higher substrate concentrations to achieve half of its maximum reaction velocity. Enzymes with high K_m values have lower efficiency in substrate binding.

8.4.3 Significance of the Michaelis Constant:

The Michaelis constant is a measure of the enzyme's efficiency in converting substrate into product. Enzymes with lower K_m values are more efficient at catalysing reactions. K_m provides important insights into the physiological role of enzymes and their interactions with substrates in biological systems. Knowledge of K_m is crucial for understanding enzyme-substrate interactions, designing enzyme assays, and optimizing enzymatic processes in biotechnological and pharmaceutical applications.

8.4.4 Maximum Reaction Velocity (V_{max}):

The maximum reaction velocity (V_{max}) is a fundamental parameter in enzyme kinetics that represents the maximum rate at which an enzyme-catalysed reaction can proceed when all enzyme active sites are saturated with substrate. It is one of the key parameters used to characterize enzyme activity and is a crucial parameter in the Michaelis-Menten equation.

8.4.4.1 Definition:

V_{max} is the rate of the reaction when the enzyme is fully saturated with substrate, and the enzyme-substrate complex is formed at its maximum possible rate. At V_{max}, the enzyme is operating at its maximal capacity, and further increases in substrate concentration will not lead to an increase in the reaction rate.

8.4.4.2 Mathematical Representation:

In the Michaelis-Menten equation, V_{max} is the asymptotic value of the reaction velocity (V) as the substrate concentration ($[S]$) becomes very large:

$$V_{max} = lim_{[S] \to \infty} V$$

8.4.4.3 Interpretation:

V_{max} reflects the intrinsic catalytic efficiency of the enzyme, representing the rate at which the enzyme can convert substrate into product when fully saturated with substrate. It is a measure of the enzyme's turnover number (k_{cat}), which represents the number of substrate molecules converted into product per enzyme active site per unit time when the enzyme is fully saturated with substrate. V_{max} is influenced by factors such as enzyme concentration, enzyme purity, temperature, pH, and the presence of inhibitors or activators.

8.4.4.4 Practical Implications:

Determining V_{max} experimentally is essential for characterizing enzyme kinetics and understanding the enzyme's catalytic properties. V_{max} provides valuable information about the enzyme's functional capacity and its potential in various biotechnological and industrial applications. Knowledge of V_{max} is crucial for enzyme assay design, enzyme purification, enzyme engineering, and the development of enzyme-based therapeutics or biocatalysts.

8.4.5 Catalytic Efficiency (k_{cat}/K_m):

Catalytic efficiency is a measure of an enzyme's effectiveness in catalysing a specific reaction, often quantified by the ratio of the enzyme's turnover number (k_{cat}) to its Michaelis constant (K_m). It provides valuable information about the enzyme's ability to convert substrate molecules into products and is a key parameter in enzyme kinetics and biochemical studies.

8.4.5.1 Mathematical Representation:

Catalytic efficiency is calculated as the ratio of the enzyme's turnover number ($k$cat) to its Michaelis constant (K_m):

$$\text{Catalytic Efficiency} = \frac{k_{cat}}{K_m}$$

Where:

- k_{cat} (turnover number) = the number of catalytic cycles per second, also calculated as $\frac{V_{max}}{[E]}$, where [E] is the enzyme concentration.

- K_m = Michaelis constant, representing the substrate concentration at $\frac{V_{max}}{2}$.

A higher catalytic efficiency indicates that the enzyme can convert substrate into product more rapidly and with greater efficiency. Catalytic efficiency combines both kinetic parameters (k_{cat} and K_m) to provide a comprehensive measure of the enzyme's performance. Enzymes with high catalytic efficiency have high turnover numbers (k_{cat}) and/or low Michaelis constants (K_m), indicating rapid substrate turnover and/or high substrate affinity.

8.4.5.3 Practical Implications:

Catalytic efficiency is a critical parameter for evaluating and comparing the performance of different enzymes in catalysing specific reactions. It provides insights into the enzyme's functional capacity, substrate specificity, and suitability for various biotechnological and industrial applications. Understanding the catalytic efficiency of enzymes is essential for enzyme engineering, rational enzyme design, and the optimization of enzymatic processes in biocatalysis, drug discovery, and other fields.

CHAPTER IX

Factors Affecting Enzyme Activity

Enzyme activity is influenced by a variety of factors that determine the rate and efficiency of catalysis, making it a central area of study in biochemistry. Key factors include temperature, pH, substrate concentration, enzyme concentration, and the presence of inhibitors or activators, all of which can significantly alter enzyme function. These parameters shape the enzyme's ability to facilitate reactions under different physiological and environmental conditions. Recent research has shed light on the impact of protein dynamics and structural flexibility on enzyme activity, revealing how subtle changes in an enzyme's conformation can influence its catalytic properties. Additionally, advancements in enzyme engineering have enabled scientists to modulate enzyme activity by designing enzymes with optimized properties for industrial and therapeutic applications. Understanding these factors is essential for leveraging enzymes in biotechnology, medicine, and agriculture.

9.1 Temperature:

Temperature plays a critical role in regulating enzyme activity, profoundly influencing the rate of enzymatic reactions and overall biological processes. Enzymes, being protein molecules, have optimal temperature ranges within which they function most efficiently. Deviations from this optimal temperature can significantly impact the enzyme's structure and its ability to catalyse reactions. Both increases and decreases in temperature can alter reaction rates, affect the stability of enzyme-substrate complexes, and ultimately determine the enzyme's effectiveness in carrying out biological functions. Understanding the relationship between temperature and enzyme activity is crucial for comprehending various physiological processes and for optimizing industrial applications that involve enzymes. Here's a detailed explanation of how temperature affects enzyme activity:

9.1.1. Molecular Motion and Collision Frequency:

As temperature increases, the kinetic energy of molecules rises, leading to greater molecular motion and more frequent collisions between enzymes and substrates. Enzymes catalyse reactions by positioning substrates in the correct orientation and lowering the activation energy required for the reaction to proceed. Higher temperatures enhance the likelihood of successful enzyme-substrate interactions, thus increasing the reaction rate. However, extreme temperatures can lead to enzyme denaturation, where the enzyme's structure is disrupted, resulting in a loss of catalytic activity. Recent studies highlight the role of protein flexibility at elevated temperatures, revealing that while moderate heat can optimize enzyme performance, excessive heat may destabilize essential interactions within the enzyme's active site, impairing function.

9.1.2. Optimal Temperature:

Each enzyme has an optimal temperature at which it exhibits maximum activity, usually near the physiological temperature of the organism in which it operates (Figure 1). At this optimal temperature, the enzyme's active site maintains its most functional conformation, enabling efficient substrate binding and catalysis. A list of the enzymes with their optimum temperature is given in Table 1. The reaction rate is highest at this point because the balance between molecular motion and enzyme stability is ideal, promoting rapid enzymatic turnover. Deviations from the optimal temperature can reduce enzyme activity, either by slowing molecular interactions at lower temperatures or by causing structural denaturation at higher temperatures, leading to a decline in catalytic efficiency.

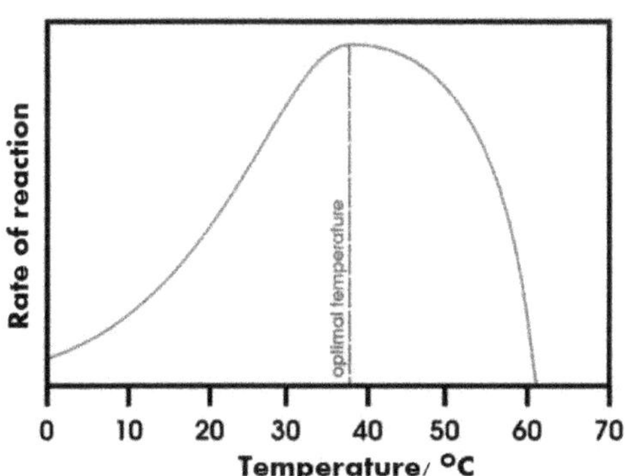

Figure 1 Optimal temperature curve for enzymatic activity

Table 1 List of enzymes with the optimum

Enzyme	Optimum Temperature (°C)	Substrate	Function
Amylase	37°C	Starch	Breaks down starch into simpler sugars (maltose).
Pepsin	37-42°C	Proteins	Digests proteins into peptides in the stomach.
Lipase	37°C	Lipids (fats)	Catalyses the breakdown of fats into fatty acids and glycerol.
Lactase	37°C	Lactose	Breaks down lactose into glucose and galactose.
Catalase	30-40°C	Hydrogen peroxide	Decomposes hydrogen peroxide into water and oxygen.
DNA Polymerase	72°C	Nucleotides	Synthesizes new DNA strands during replication.
Urease	60°C	Urea	Converts urea into ammonia and carbon dioxide.
Trypsin	37°C	Proteins	Breaks down proteins into smaller peptides in the small intestine.
Cellulase	50-60°C	Cellulose	Breaks down cellulose into glucose monomers.
Taq Polymerase	75-80°C	Nucleotides	Synthesizes DNA at high temperatures during PCR.

9.1.3. Denaturation at High Temperatures:

Excessively high temperatures can denature enzymes, causing them to lose their three-dimensional structure and, consequently, their biological activity. This denaturation process disrupts the non-covalent interactions, such as hydrogen bonds and hydrophobic interactions, that stabilize the enzyme's tertiary and quaternary structures, leading to the unfolding of the enzyme and a loss of its functional integrity. As a result, denatured enzymes can no longer bind substrates effectively or catalyse reactions, leading to a significant reduction or complete loss of enzymatic activity.

Recent research has shown that certain engineered enzymes and thermostable variants can resist denaturation at elevated temperatures, making them valuable in industrial processes that require high-temperature conditions.

9.1.4. Temperature Coefficient (Q_{10}):

The temperature coefficient (Q_{10}) is a measure that quantifies the rate of change in enzyme activity with a 10-degree Celsius increase in temperature. It is calculated as the ratio of the reaction rate at a higher temperature to the rate at a lower temperature. For most enzymatic reactions, the Q_{10} value typically ranges between 2 and 3, meaning that enzyme activity roughly doubles or triples with every 10°C increase, as long as the temperature remains within the enzyme's physiological range. This phenomenon highlights the sensitivity of enzymes to temperature changes, promoting faster reaction rates. However, beyond the optimal range, enzyme activity can decline due to denaturation. Recent studies have utilized the Q_{10} value to optimize enzyme performance in industrial and medical applications, where precise temperature control is critical for maintaining enzymatic efficiency.

9.1.5. Adaptation to Extreme Temperatures:

Some organisms, particularly extremophiles, have evolved enzymes that are adapted to function under extreme temperature conditions, either at high temperatures in thermophiles or low temperatures in psychrophiles. Thermophilic enzymes are highly stable and maintain their activity at elevated temperatures, making them ideal for industrial processes that require heat-resistant catalysts. On the other hand, psychrophilic enzymes are optimized for cold environments, exhibiting enhanced flexibility to catalyse reactions efficiently at low temperatures. These adaptations involve specific modifications in enzyme structure and composition, such as increased thermostability in thermophiles through stronger intramolecular bonds or enhanced flexibility in psychrophiles to compensate for reduced molecular motion. Recent research into extremophilic enzymes has led to their application in various biotechnological fields, including biofuel production and bioremediation in extreme environmental conditions.

9.1.6. Temperature-Dependent Kinetics:

Changes in temperature can affect enzyme kinetics, altering parameters such as the Michaelis constant (K_m) and maximum reaction rate (V_{max}). At higher temperatures, enzyme-substrate binding may become less specific (increased K_m), while the rate of the catalytic reaction may increase (increased V_{max}). These temperature-dependent changes in enzyme kinetics can impact the overall efficiency and specificity of enzymatic reactions under different temperature conditions.

9.2 pH:

pH plays a crucial role in regulating enzyme activity, as it directly influences the ionization state of amino acid residues within the enzyme's active site. This ionization, in turn, affects the enzyme's ability to bind substrates and catalyse reactions. Each enzyme operates optimally within a specific pH range, and deviations from this optimal pH can lead to changes in the charge of the active site, reducing the enzyme's catalytic efficiency. Extreme pH levels may even result in denaturation of the enzyme, rendering it inactive. Understanding the relationship between pH and enzyme activity is essential for both biological systems and industrial applications where precise enzymatic control is required. Here's a detailed explanation of how pH affects enzyme activity:

9.2.1. Optimal pH:

Each enzyme has an optimal pH range at which it exhibits maximum activity, determined by the ionization states of the specific amino acid residues within its active site. These residues must maintain the correct charge and configuration to effectively bind substrates and catalyse reactions. The optimal pH (Figure 2) for an enzyme is typically close to the physiological pH of the organism or the cellular compartment where it operates. Deviations from this pH range can alter the enzyme's structure and function, reducing its catalytic efficiency. Understanding the optimal pH is critical for applications in drug design, industrial enzyme usage, and metabolic engineering. A list of enzymes with their optimum pH is given in Table 2.

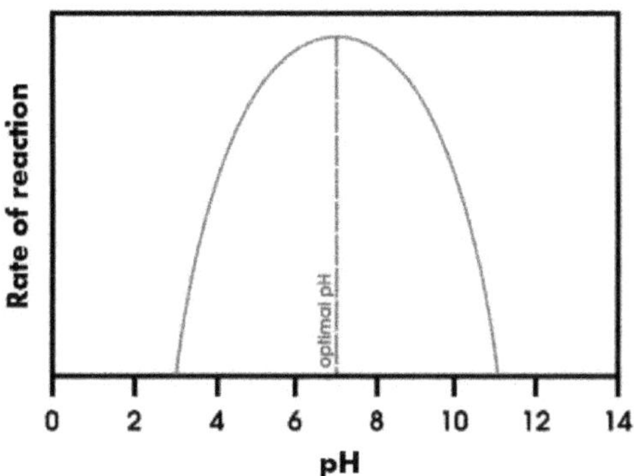

Figure 2Optimal pH curve for enzymatic activity

Table 2 List of enzymes with their optimum pH

Enzyme	Optimum pH	Example of Substrate	Working Function
Pepsin	1.5 - 2.0	Proteins	Breaks down proteins into peptides in the stomach.
Trypsin	7.5 - 8.5	Proteins	Digests proteins into peptides and amino acids in the small intestine.
Amylase	6.7 - 7.0	Starch	Converts starch into maltose in saliva and the small intestine.
Lipase	8	Triglycerides	Breaks down triglycerides into fatty acids and glycerol in the small intestine.
Lactase	6	Lactose	Converts lactose into glucose and galactose in the small intestine.
Phosphatase	9.0 - 10.0	Phosphate esters	Removes phosphate groups from molecules in various tissues.
Carbonic Anhydrase	7.0 - 7.5	Carbon dioxide	Catalyses the reversible hydration of carbon dioxide in blood.
Hexokinase	7	Glucose	Converts glucose into glucose-6-phosphate in glycolysis.
Arginase	9.5 - 10.5	Arginine	Converts arginine into urea and ornithine in the urea cycle.

9.2.2. Effect of pH on Enzyme Structure:

Changes in pH can disrupt the three-dimensional structure of enzymes, especially in the active site region, where precise interactions are crucial for catalysis. The ionization states of amino acid residues, particularly acidic residues like aspartate and glutamate, and basic residues such as lysine and histidine, are highly sensitive to pH changes. Deviations from the optimal pH can result in the protonation or deprotonation of these residues, altering their charge and disturbing the electrostatic interactions that maintain the enzyme's active conformation. This disruption can lead to reduced substrate binding and catalytic activity, highlighting the importance of maintaining the appropriate pH for optimal enzyme function.

9.2.3. Disruption of Ionic Bonds:

Ionic interactions between charged amino acid residues within an enzyme's active site and the substrate are essential for effective substrate binding and catalysis. These interactions help stabilize the enzyme-substrate complex, ensuring proper orientation for the reaction to occur. Changes in pH can disrupt these ionic bonds by altering the ionization states of the involved residues, such as acidic or basic side chains, thereby affecting the enzyme's conformation. This disruption can lead to reduced substrate-binding affinity and diminished catalytic efficiency, making pH regulation critical for maintaining enzyme functionality in various physiological and industrial settings.

9.2.4. Alteration of Enzyme Activity:

Deviations from the optimal pH can significantly reduce enzyme activity by decreasing substrate-binding affinity, altering catalytic efficiency, or even causing enzyme denaturation. At pH values outside the optimal range, the enzyme's structure may become destabilized, compromising the integrity of its active site. This destabilization disrupts essential interactions required for effective catalysis, leading to a sharp decline in enzyme activity. In extreme cases, prolonged exposure to unsuitable pH conditions can result in irreversible structural changes, rendering the enzyme inactive. Understanding and maintaining the optimal pH is therefore critical for preserving enzyme functionality in both biological and industrial processes.

9.2.5. pH-Dependent Kinetics:

Changes in pH can also affect enzyme kinetics, altering parameters such as the Michaelis constant (K_m) and maximum reaction rate (V_{max}). At pH values outside the optimal range, enzyme-substrate binding may become less specific (increased K_m), while the rate of the catalytic reaction may decrease (decreased V_{max}).

9.2.6. pH Regulation in Biological Systems:

Biological systems tightly regulate pH to ensure optimal conditions for enzyme activity and overall cellular function. Intracellular enzymes are adapted to function at specific pH values that correspond to the pH of the cellular compartments in which they operate, such as the cytoplasm or lysosomes. For example, enzymes in lysosomes have an acidic pH optimum, while those in the cytoplasm typically function near neutral pH. Buffer systems, like phosphate buffers in cells and bicarbonate buffers in blood, play a crucial role in stabilizing pH, preventing fluctuations that could disrupt enzyme activity. These systems help maintain enzymatic efficiency and support vital metabolic processes within physiological pH ranges.

9.3 Substrate Concentration:

Substrate concentration profoundly influences enzyme activity, dictating the rate at which enzymatic reactions proceed. As the concentration of substrate increases, the reaction rate initially rises due to more frequent enzyme-substrate collisions. However, beyond a certain point, the enzyme's active sites become saturated, and the reaction rate reaches a maximum velocity (V_{ax}). At this stage, increasing substrate concentration further has no effect on the reaction rate. This relationship between substrate concentration and enzyme activity is a key concept in enzyme kinetics, helping to explain how enzymes function efficiently under varying conditions. Here's a detailed explanation of how substrate concentration impacts enzyme activity:

9.3.1. Limitation by Substrate Availability:

At low substrate concentrations, enzyme activity is restricted by the limited availability of substrate molecules. Enzymes can only catalyse reactions when substrate molecules bind to their active sites, forming enzyme-substrate complexes. When substrates are scarce, fewer of these complexes form, resulting in a lower rate of reaction. Under such conditions, many enzymes may remain idle or exhibit minimal activity, waiting for substrate molecules to become available. This relationship between substrate availability and enzyme activity is a fundamental aspect of enzyme kinetics, particularly evident in environments where substrates fluctuate, such as in metabolic regulation.

9.3.2. Saturation of Enzyme Active Sites:

As substrate concentration increases, the rate of enzyme activity typically rises proportionally, as more substrate molecules bind to the available enzyme active sites. However, once all active sites are occupied, the enzyme reaches saturation, meaning that every enzyme molecule is engaged in catalysis. At this saturation point, further increases in substrate concentration do not lead to a corresponding rise in reaction rate. The enzyme has reached its maximum reaction rate, known as V_{max}, and the reaction is said to be operating at maximum velocity. This concept is fundamental in enzyme kinetics, illustrating that enzyme activity is limited by the availability of active sites, even if more substrate is present.

9.3.3. Michaelis-Menten Kinetics:

The relationship between substrate concentration and enzyme activity is described by the Michaelis-Menten equation, which models the kinetics of enzyme-catalysed reactions. At low substrate concentrations, the rate of the enzymatic reaction is directly proportional to the substrate concentration, following first-order kinetics, where the reaction rate increases linearly with the amount of substrate available. As the substrate concentration rises and approaches saturation, the reaction rate nears its maximum velocity (V_{max}), and the reaction transitions to zero-order kinetics. At this point, the reaction rate becomes independent of substrate concentration, as all enzyme active sites are occupied, and the enzyme is operating at full capacity.

9.3.4. Determination of K_m:

The Michaelis constant (K_m) is a measure of the enzyme's affinity for its substrate and is defined as the substrate concentration at which the reaction rate is half of V_{max}. K_m reflects the enzyme's ability to bind substrate molecules and is inversely related to substrate affinity: enzymes with lower K_m values have higher substrate affinity. At substrate concentrations much lower than K_m, the enzyme is substrate-limited, and the reaction rate is proportional to substrate concentration. At substrate concentrations much higher than K_m, the enzyme is saturated with substrate, and the reaction rate approaches V_{max}.

9.3.5. Practical Implications:

Understanding the relationship between substrate concentration and enzyme activity is essential for optimizing enzymatic reactions in fields like biotechnology, pharmaceuticals, and biochemistry. By varying substrate concentrations in enzyme assays, researchers can determine key kinetic parameters such as K_m and V_{max}, which offer valuable insights into an enzyme's affinity for its substrate and its catalytic efficiency. These parameters are critical for tailoring enzyme usage in industrial processes, drug development, and metabolic studies, enabling precise control over reaction conditions to maximize efficiency and specificity.

9.4 Enzyme Inhibitors:

Enzyme inhibitors are molecules that bind to enzymes and reduce their activity, thereby modulating biochemical pathways and cellular processes. There are two main types of enzyme inhibitors: competitive and non-competitive inhibitors. Here's a detailed explanation of each type:

9.4.1. Competitive Inhibition:

Competitive inhibitors are molecules that resemble the substrate and compete for binding to the enzyme's active site. These inhibitors often share a similar structure with the substrate and can bind either reversibly or irreversibly to the active site. When a competitive inhibitor occupies the active site, it prevents the substrate from binding, thereby reducing the formation of enzyme-substrate complexes and inhibiting the catalytic process. However, competitive inhibition can be overcome by increasing the concentration of the substrate, which allows the substrate to outcompete the inhibitor for active site binding. The presence of a competitive inhibitor raises the apparent K_m of the enzyme, indicating that higher substrate concentrations are needed to reach half of the maximum reaction velocity ($V_{max}/2$) in the presence of the inhibitor, although V_{max} itself remains unchanged.

9.4.2. Non-competitive Inhibition:

Non-competitive inhibitors bind to sites on the enzyme other than the active site, known as allosteric sites. The binding of the non-competitive inhibitor induces conformational changes in the enzyme, altering its active site and reducing its catalytic activity. Non-competitive inhibitors can bind to both the enzyme-substrate complex and the free enzyme, affecting both substrate binding and catalysis. Unlike competitive inhibition, increasing the concentration of the substrate cannot overcome non-competitive inhibition, as the inhibitor binds to a different site on the enzyme. Non-competitive inhibition does not affect the apparent K_m of the enzyme but reduces the maximum reaction rate (V_{max}) by decreasing the number of active enzyme molecules available for catalysis.

9.4.3. Reversibility:

Both competitive and non-competitive inhibition can be either reversible or irreversible, depending on the inhibitor's nature and its binding affinity for the enzyme. Reversible inhibitors bind to the enzyme through non-covalent interactions, such as hydrogen bonds or hydrophobic interactions, and can dissociate, allowing the enzyme to regain its activity once the inhibitor is removed. In contrast, irreversible inhibitors form covalent bonds with the enzyme, resulting in permanent inhibition of enzyme activity. These inhibitors often modify key amino acid residues in the active site, rendering the enzyme inactive and unable to catalyse reactions, which makes irreversible inhibition particularly significant in drug development and toxin studies.

9.4.4. Therapeutic Applications:

Enzyme inhibitors play a crucial role in therapeutic applications and are commonly used as medications to treat a wide range of diseases and disorders. Pharmaceutical drugs often target specific enzymes that are involved in disease processes, aiming to inhibit their activity to reduce harmful effects or enhance their function to restore normal physiological balance. For instance, enzyme inhibitors are used in managing conditions like hypertension, cancer, and infections. Understanding the mechanisms of enzyme inhibition is fundamental for the rational design of drugs with optimal efficacy, allowing for the development of treatments that maximize therapeutic benefits while minimizing potential side effects. This knowledge is pivotal in modern drug discovery and development.

CHAPTER X

Allosteric Regulation of Enzymes

Enzyme regulation is a critical aspect of cellular control, ensuring that metabolic processes occur at appropriate rates and in response to the organism's needs. Through various mechanisms, cells modulate enzyme activity to maintain homeostasis, respond to environmental changes, and optimize energy usage. Enzymes can be regulated at multiple levels, including gene expression, post-translational modifications, and the action of inhibitors or activators. Additionally, allosteric regulation, feedback inhibition, and covalent modifications play key roles in fine-tuning enzymatic functions. Understanding enzyme regulation is essential for comprehending how biological pathways are controlled and how dysregulation can lead to diseases or metabolic imbalances.

10.1 Allosteric Regulation:

Allosteric regulation is a fundamental mechanism by which enzymes adjust their activity in response to changes in cellular conditions, such as the presence of specific molecules or environmental factors. In this process, regulatory molecules bind to allosteric sites on the enzyme, which are separate from the active site where substrate binding and catalysis occur. The binding of these regulatory molecules induces conformational changes in the enzyme's structure, thereby modifying its catalytic activity. This alteration can either enhance enzyme activity, known as positive allosteric regulation or inhibit it, termed negative allosteric regulation, depending on the nature of the regulatory molecule and its effect on the enzyme's conformation. Through these conformational adjustments, allosteric regulation allows for precise control over enzymatic reactions, enabling the enzyme to adapt to varying metabolic needs and environmental conditions.

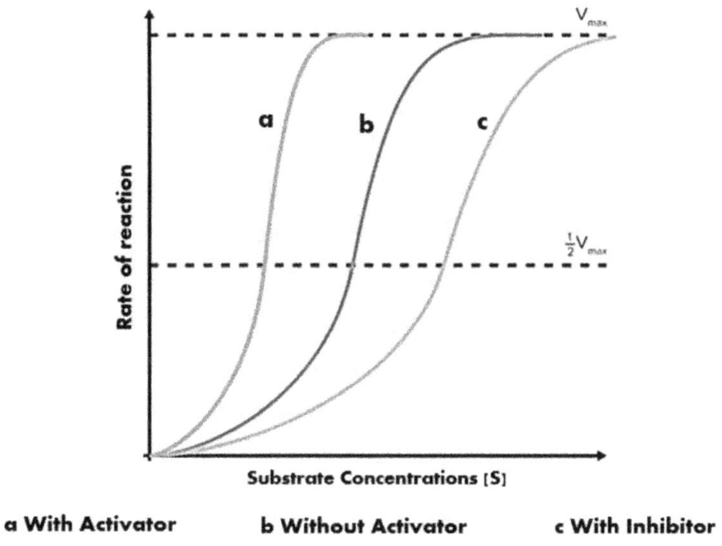

Figure 1 Effect of allosteric regulation on the enzyme activity

10.2 Features of Allosteric Regulation:

10.2.1 Allosteric Sites:

Allosteric regulation involves the binding of regulatory molecules to allosteric sites on the enzyme, which are distinct from the active site where substrate binding and catalysis occur. These allosteric sites can be situated on different subunits of multimeric enzymes or separate domains within the enzyme's structure. The binding of a regulatory molecule to an allosteric site induces conformational changes in the enzyme, which can either enhance or inhibit its catalytic activity. This spatial separation between the allosteric site and the active site allows for intricate control over enzyme function, enabling the enzyme to respond to changes in cellular conditions and regulate metabolic pathways effectively.

10.2.2 Conformational Changes:

The binding of a regulatory molecule to the allosteric site induces conformational changes in the enzyme's structure, leading to alterations in its catalytic activity. These conformational shifts can influence the enzyme's affinity for its substrates, potentially increasing or decreasing how tightly substrates bind to the active site. Additionally, the changes can affect the enzyme's catalytic rate, either enhancing or reducing the efficiency with which it converts substrates into products. By modulating these aspects of enzyme function, allosteric regulation provides a mechanism for fine-tuning enzymatic activity in response to fluctuations in cellular conditions or the presence of specific regulatory molecules.

10.2.3 Positive and Negative Regulation:

Allosteric regulation can either enhance or inhibit enzyme activity depending on the nature of the regulatory molecule and its interaction with the enzyme. In positive allosteric regulation, the binding of a regulatory molecule to the allosteric site increases the enzyme's activity. This often occurs by inducing conformational changes that enhance the enzyme's affinity for its substrate or increase its catalytic efficiency. Conversely, in negative allosteric regulation, the binding of a regulatory molecule decreases the enzyme's activity. This is typically achieved by conformational changes that reduce the enzyme's affinity for its substrate or inhibit its catalytic function. The effects of allosteric regulation are directly mediated by the structural adjustments in the enzyme induced by the binding of the regulatory molecule, thereby fine-tuning enzymatic activity in response to cellular needs and environmental conditions.

10.2.4 Cooperative Binding:

Allosteric enzymes often exhibit cooperative binding behaviour, a phenomenon where the binding of one substrate molecule to the enzyme influences the binding of additional substrate molecules. This cooperative effect typically results in sigmoidal (S-shaped) saturation curves in enzyme kinetics plots, as opposed to the hyperbolic saturation curves seen with non-allosteric enzymes. In cooperative binding, the initial substrate binding induces conformational changes in the enzyme that enhance the affinity of additional substrate binding sites, leading to a more pronounced increase in reaction rate as substrate concentration increases. This behaviour reflects the dynamic and cooperative nature of allosteric regulation, highlighting the enzyme's ability to integrate multiple regulatory signals and modulate its activity accordingly.

10.2.5 Feedback Inhibition:

Allosteric regulation plays a critical role in feedback inhibition, a fundamental regulatory mechanism in metabolic pathways. In feedback inhibition, the end product of a metabolic pathway binds to an allosteric site on an enzyme that operates earlier in the pathway. This binding induces a conformational change in the enzyme, reducing its activity and thereby regulating the overall flux through the pathway. By inhibiting the enzyme, feedback inhibition prevents the overproduction of the end product, ensuring that the metabolic pathway operates efficiently and maintains homeostasis within the cell. This mechanism allows cells to fine-tune metabolic processes in response to varying levels of metabolites and other regulatory signals.

10.3 Allosteric Enzymes:

Many enzymes involved in key metabolic pathways, such as phosphofructokinase, glycogen phosphorylase, and pyruvate kinase, are subject to allosteric regulation, which enables precise control of metabolic flux in response to fluctuating cellular conditions and demands. Allosteric enzymes possess regulatory sites distinct from their active sites, where molecules such as activators or inhibitors can bind. This binding induces conformational changes that either enhance or inhibit the enzyme's activity. For instance, **phosphofructokinase**, a rate-limiting enzyme in glycolysis, is allosterically inhibited by high levels of ATP (signalling abundant energy) and activated by AMP (indicating low energy availability). Similarly, **glycogen phosphorylase**, involved in glycogen breakdown, is allosterically activated by AMP when energy is required. These regulatory mechanisms ensure that metabolic pathways are dynamically adjusted to meet the cell's energy requirements, preventing the wasteful use of resources and maintaining metabolic balance under varying physiological conditions.

Table 1 Examples of enzymes, their allosteric inhibitors, activators, and the reactions they catalyse

Enzyme	Allosteric Inhibitor(s)	Allosteric Activator(s)	Reaction Catalysed
Phosphofructokinase-1 (PFK-1)	ATP, Citrate	AMP, ADP, Fructose-2,6-bisphosphate	Conversion of fructose-6-phosphate to fructose-1,6-bisphosphate in glycolysis
Pyruvate kinase	ATP, Acetyl-CoA	Fructose-1,6-bisphosphate	Conversion of phosphoenolpyruvate (PEP) to pyruvate in glycolysis
Glycogen phosphorylase	ATP, Glucose-6-phosphate	AMP, ADP	Catalyses the release of glucose-1-phosphate from glycogen
Aspartate transcarbamoylase (ATCase)	CTP	ATP	Catalyses the first step in the pyrimidine biosynthesis pathway
Isocitrate dehydrogenase	ATP, NADH	ADP, NAD+	Oxidative decarboxylation of isocitrate to alpha-ketoglutarate in the citric acid cycle
Acetyl-CoA carboxylase (ACC)	Palmitoyl-CoA, AMP	Citrate	Catalyses the carboxylation of acetyl-CoA to malonyl-CoA in fatty acid biosynthesis
Glutamate dehydrogenase	GTP, ATP	ADP, Leucine	Conversion of glutamate to alpha-ketoglutarate and ammonia
Threonine deaminase	Isoleucine	Valine	Conversion of threonine to alpha-ketobutyrate in the biosynthesis of isoleucine
Carbamoyl phosphate synthetase II	UTP	ATP, PRPP	Synthesis of carbamoyl phosphate from glutamine and bicarbonate in pyrimidine biosynthesis
Phosphoenolpyruvate carboxylase (PEPCase)	Malate	Glucose-6-phosphate	Catalyses the conversion of phosphoenolpyruvate to oxaloacetate in C4 plants

10.4 Allosteric Activators:

Allosteric activators (Table 1) are regulatory molecules that bind to specific sites on enzymes known as allosteric sites, distinct from the enzyme's active site. Unlike substrates, which bind to the active site and are converted into products, allosteric activators do not participate directly in the chemical reaction. Instead, they bind to these allosteric sites and induce conformational changes in the enzyme's structure. These conformational changes enhance the enzyme's catalytic activity, often by increasing the enzyme's affinity for its substrate or by altering the enzyme's overall conformation to favour the catalytic process. This mechanism of allosteric activation is crucial for the regulation of enzyme activity in response to cellular signals or metabolic conditions, allowing cells to finely tune biochemical pathways and ensure efficient and responsive control over various cellular processes.

Allosteric activation is characterized by several key features that collectively enhance the catalytic activity of enzymes. Allosteric activators bind to specific allosteric sites on enzymes, which are distinct from the enzyme's active site and may be located on different subunits of multimeric enzymes or separate domains within the enzyme structure. This binding induces conformational changes in the enzyme, stabilizing an active conformation that enhances its catalytic activity. These structural adjustments can increase the enzyme's affinity for substrates, improve catalytic turnover rates, or both. Allosteric activators exert positive regulation by enhancing the rate of the enzymatic reaction through mechanisms that may include binding to allosteric sites or inducing post-translational modifications. Additionally, allosteric activators may exhibit cooperative binding behaviour, where the binding of one activator molecule facilitates the binding of subsequent activators, leading to sigmoidal saturation curves in enzyme kinetics plots. This cooperative effect is indicative of positive cooperativity. The physiological significance of allosteric activation lies in its crucial role in regulating metabolic pathways, signal transduction cascades, and various cellular processes. By enabling precise modulation of enzyme activity in response to specific signals or metabolic cues, allosteric activation allows cells to adapt efficiently to changing environmental conditions or metabolic demands.

10.5 Examples of Allosteric Activation:

10.5.1 Phosphofructokinase-1 (PFK-1):

Phosphofructokinase-1 (PFK-1), a critical regulatory enzyme in glycolysis, is allosterically activated by fructose-2,6-bisphosphate (F2,6BP), a potent activator that fine-tunes glycolytic flux. F2,6BP binds to an allosteric site on PFK-1, triggering conformational changes that enhance the enzyme's catalytic activity. This activation promotes the conversion of glucose to pyruvate, accelerating glycolysis and increasing the cell's energy production. By stimulating PFK-1 activity, F2,6BP plays a crucial role in regulating glycolytic flux in response to hormonal signals and cellular metabolic needs, ensuring efficient energy generation during periods of increased demand.

10.5.2 Aspartate Transcarbamoylase (ATCase):

Aspartate transcarbamoylase (ATCase), a key enzyme in the pyrimidine biosynthesis pathway, is allosterically activated by ATP, ensuring proper nucleotide balance for nucleic acid synthesis. ATP binds to allosteric sites on ATCase, stabilizing the enzyme in its active conformation, which enhances its catalytic activity. This activation increases the production of pyrimidine nucleotides, which are essential for DNA and RNA synthesis. By linking pyrimidine biosynthesis to ATP levels, the cell coordinates nucleotide production with energy availability, promoting nucleic acid synthesis during periods of high metabolic activity and cell growth.

10.5.3 Haemoglobin:

Haemoglobin, a tetrameric protein responsible for oxygen transport in the blood, exhibits allosteric activation through its oxygen-binding mechanism. When oxygen binds to one of its four subunits, it induces conformational changes in the haemoglobin structure, making it easier for oxygen to bind to the remaining subunits. This process, known as positive cooperativity, enhances haemoglobin's overall oxygen-binding capacity. Through this allosteric activation, haemoglobin efficiently picks up oxygen in the lungs and releases it in tissues, allowing for precise oxygen delivery in response to the body's physiological needs.

10.6 Allosteric Inhibitors:

Allosteric inhibitors (Table 1) are regulatory molecules that bind to allosteric sites on enzymes, distinct from the active site, and decrease their catalytic activity by inducing conformational changes in the enzyme's structure. Unlike competitive inhibitors, which directly compete with substrates for the active site, allosteric inhibitors bind to separate sites on the enzyme, modulating its activity indirectly. This binding alters the enzyme's conformation in a way that reduces its ability to catalyse reactions, thereby affecting its overall catalytic efficiency. Allosteric inhibition is a vital regulatory mechanism that enables cells to respond to specific cellular signals or metabolic conditions by fine-tuning enzyme activity. This form of regulation helps maintain metabolic homeostasis and ensures that biochemical pathways are appropriately modulated in response to changing environmental or internal conditions. By adjusting enzyme activity through allosteric inhibition, cells can effectively control the rates of biochemical reactions and adapt to fluctuations in substrate concentrations or other physiological signals.

Allosteric inhibitors are regulatory molecules that bind to distinct allosteric sites on enzymes, which are separate from the active site where substrate binding occurs. These allosteric sites can be located on different subunits of multimeric enzymes or on separate domains within the enzyme structure. The binding of allosteric inhibitors induces conformational changes in the enzyme's structure, stabilizing an inactive conformation that reduces its catalytic activity. This alteration can decrease the enzyme's affinity for substrates and lower catalytic turnover rates, effectively inhibiting the enzymatic reaction. Allosteric inhibition exerts negative regulation on enzyme activity, which can occur through mechanisms distinct from those of competitive inhibition, such as binding to non-active sites or through post-translational modifications. Often, allosteric inhibition is involved in feedback regulation of metabolic pathways, where inhibitors bind to specific enzymes in the pathway to control the flux of metabolites and prevent the overaccumulation of intermediates or end products. This form of regulation is crucial for maintaining metabolic homeostasis, as it allows cells to adjust their biochemical activity in response to changes in environmental conditions or metabolic demands. By modulating enzyme activity through allosteric inhibition, cells can precisely control their metabolic processes and ensure efficient adaptation to varying physiological needs.

10.6.1 Example of Allosteric Inhibition:

10.6.1.1 Phosphofructokinase-1 (PFK-1):

Phosphofructokinase-1 (PFK-1), a key regulatory enzyme in glycolysis, is allosterically inhibited by ATP, playing a crucial role in cellular energy regulation. ATP binds to specific allosteric sites on PFK-1, causing conformational changes that stabilize the enzyme in an inactive form, thus reducing its catalytic activity. This allosteric inhibition acts as a feedback mechanism to control glycolytic flux in response to cellular energy levels. When ATP levels are high, this inhibition slows down glycolysis, preventing the unnecessary breakdown of glucose and conserving energy for future needs. This regulatory process ensures that glycolysis is tightly controlled, aligning energy production with cellular demand.

CHAPTER XI

Enzyme Inhibition

Enzyme inhibition is a fundamental concept in enzymology and biochemistry that plays a crucial role in regulating enzyme activity and, consequently, metabolic pathways within cells. Inhibitors are molecules that can decrease or halt the activity of enzymes, either temporarily or permanently, by binding to specific sites on the enzyme. This process is essential for maintaining cellular homeostasis, controlling metabolic flux, and responding to changes in the environment. Enzyme inhibition can be broadly categorized into reversible and irreversible types, each involving different mechanisms of interaction with the enzyme. Reversible inhibition is characterized by the non-covalent binding of inhibitors that can dissociate from the enzyme, while irreversible inhibition involves the formation of covalent bonds that permanently inactivate the enzyme. Understanding the mechanisms and effects of enzyme inhibition not only provides insights into enzyme function and regulation but also has practical implications in drug design and therapeutic intervention. This chapter delves into the various types of enzyme inhibition, their mechanisms, and their significance in both basic biological processes and applied biomedical research.

Enzyme inhibition is categorized into two main types: reversible and irreversible inhibition, each with distinct mechanisms and effects on enzyme activity. **Reversible inhibition** involves inhibitors that bind to enzymes through non-covalent interactions, and their effects can be reversed by removing the inhibitor or by increasing substrate concentration. This category includes several types: **competitive inhibition**, where the inhibitor competes with the substrate for the active site, increasing the apparent K_m without affecting V_{max}; **non-competitive inhibition**, where the inhibitor binds to an allosteric site, decreasing V_{max} without altering K_m; **uncompetitive inhibition**, where the inhibitor binds only to the enzyme-substrate complex, lowering both K_m and V_{max}; and **mixed inhibition**, where the inhibitor binds to either the enzyme or the enzyme-substrate complex, generally reducing V_{max} and altering K_m. **Irreversible inhibition**, on the other hand, involves inhibitors that form a permanent covalent bond with the enzyme, resulting in a permanent loss of enzymatic activity. This type includes **covalent modification**, where the inhibitor covalently binds to a specific amino acid residue, and **suicide inhibition (mechanism-based inhibition)**, where the inhibitor is modified by the enzyme into a reactive form that irreversibly binds to the enzyme. Irreversible inhibition cannot be reversed; new enzyme molecules must be synthesized to restore activity. Understanding these inhibition types is crucial for designing specific inhibitors for therapeutic purposes and elucidating enzyme mechanisms.

11.1 Reversible Inhibition:

Reversible inhibition is a type of enzyme inhibition in which the inhibitor binds to the enzyme temporarily, and the interaction can be reversed under specific conditions. In this form of inhibition, the inhibitor forms a non-covalent complex with the enzyme, meaning that the enzyme and inhibitor can dissociate without permanent damage to the enzyme's structure or function. This contrasts with irreversible inhibition, where the inhibitor forms a covalent bond with the enzyme, leading to permanent inactivation and loss of enzymatic activity. Reversible inhibitors are often involved in regulating metabolic processes by modulating enzyme activity in response to changing cellular conditions. These inhibitors can bind to the active site, preventing the substrate from binding (competitive inhibition), or bind to other sites, affecting enzyme function indirectly (non-competitive or uncompetitive inhibition). Reversible inhibition is key to cellular regulation, allowing enzymes to be fine-tuned without permanent deactivation, and is also a critical mechanism in the development of drugs that need to control enzyme activity without causing irreversible damage.

Reversible inhibition is characterized by non-covalent binding between the inhibitor and the enzyme, facilitated through interactions such as hydrogen bonds, van der Waals forces, and electrostatic interactions. These interactions are relatively weak compared to covalent bonds, allowing the inhibitor to dissociate from the enzyme when conditions change, such as shifts in substrate concentration or environmental factors like pH and temperature. The effect of reversible inhibitors is temporary, and the enzyme's activity can be restored once the inhibitor detaches (Figure 1). This type of inhibition plays a crucial role in the regulation of metabolic pathways, as it allows cells to modulate enzyme activity without permanently deactivating enzymes. By adjusting conditions, reversible inhibition can be fine-tuned, providing a flexible mechanism for controlling enzyme function in response to cellular needs. Additionally, many pharmaceutical agents are designed as reversible inhibitors, offering therapeutic benefits by temporarily inhibiting specific enzymes involved in disease processes without causing permanent enzyme inactivation.

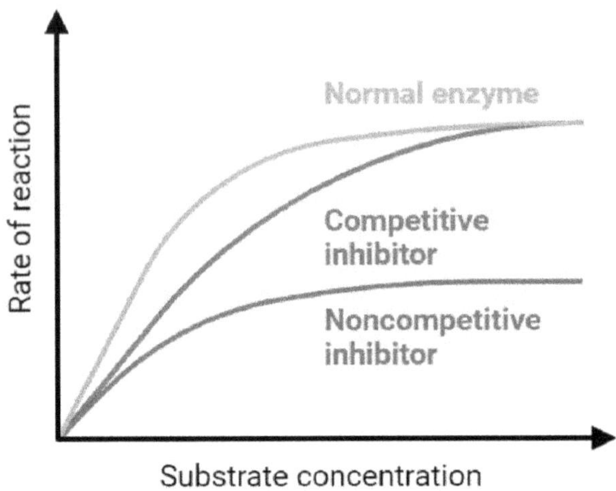

Figure 1 Effect of competitive inhibitors and non-competitive inhibitors on the rate of reaction.

11.1.1 Different Types:

Reversible inhibition can be classified into several types based on the nature of the interaction between the inhibitor and the enzyme:

11.1.1.1 Competitive Inhibition:

Competitive inhibition is a form of reversible enzyme inhibition in which the inhibitor competes directly with the substrate to bind to the enzyme's active site (Figure 3). This occurs because the inhibitor structurally resembles the substrate, allowing it to fit into the active site. When the inhibitor binds, it blocks the substrate from accessing the active site, leading to a decrease in the rate of the enzymatic reaction. However, because the binding is reversible and non-covalent, competitive inhibition can be overcome by increasing the concentration of the substrate, which increases the likelihood that the substrate will outcompete the inhibitor for active site binding. This type of inhibition does not alter the enzyme's maximum reaction velocity (V_{max}), but it increases the apparent Michaelis constant (K_m), meaning a higher substrate concentration is needed to reach half of V_{max}. Competitive inhibition is a key regulatory mechanism in many biological systems and is often exploited in drug design to develop inhibitors that target specific enzymes by mimicking the natural substrate.

Competitive inhibition is characterized by the reversible binding of an inhibitor to the active site of an enzyme, directly competing with the substrate for access. This occurs because the competitive inhibitor often has a structural resemblance to the substrate, allowing it to occupy the same binding site. However, unlike the substrate, the competitive inhibitor does not undergo a chemical reaction, and no product is formed. The inhibitory effect is reversible, as the inhibitor-enzyme complex can dissociate, allowing the enzyme to return to its active form. Competitive inhibition can be overcome by increasing the substrate concentration, which outcompetes the inhibitor for active site binding. In terms of enzyme kinetics, competitive inhibition increases the apparent K_m (Michaelis constant), meaning a higher substrate concentration is needed to reach half of the enzyme's maximum velocity, but the maximum reaction velocity (V_{max}) remains unchanged. This is evident in a Lineweaver-Burk plot, where the slope changes due to a shift in the x-axis intercept ($-1/K_m$) while the y-axis intercept ($1/V_{max}$) remains constant (Figure 2).

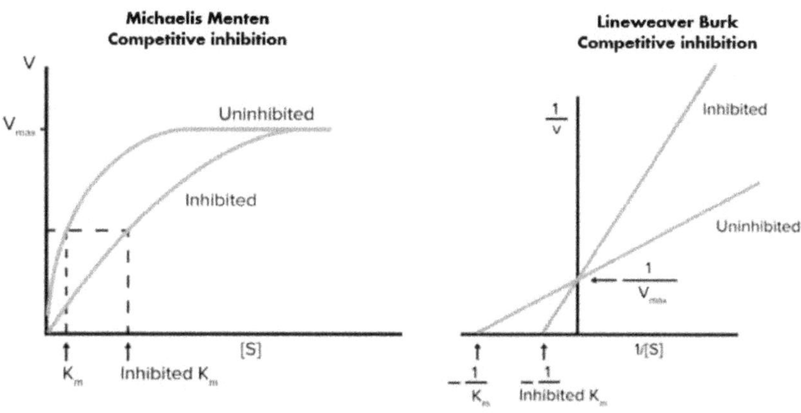

Figure 2 Effect of competitive inhibitors on the Michaelis-Menten curve and Lineweaver-Burk Plot

Competitive inhibition is highly relevant in drug design, as many therapeutic agents act as competitive inhibitors, blocking the active site of target enzymes to regulate biochemical processes. The inhibition constant (K_i) quantifies the affinity of these inhibitors for the enzyme, providing insights into their effectiveness. Competitive inhibition is also employed in biotechnological and industrial applications to control enzyme activity in various biochemical processes. Understanding its mechanisms is essential for studying enzyme kinetics and optimizing processes in both research and applied fields.

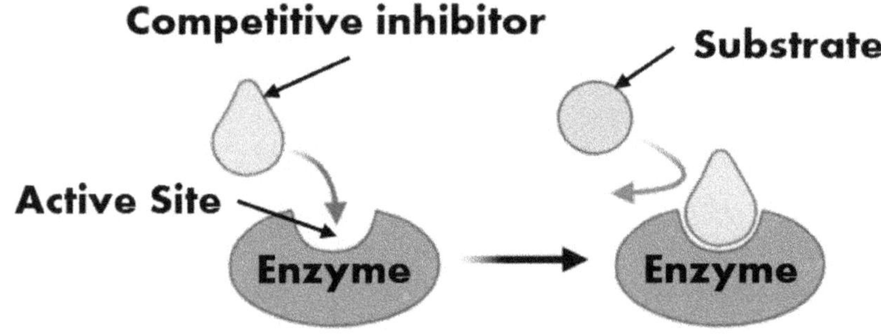

Figure 3 Mechanism of competitive inhibition

11.1.1.2 Non-competitive Inhibition:
Non-competitive inhibition (Figure 4) is a form of reversible enzyme inhibition in which the inhibitor binds to an allosteric site on the enzyme, separate from the active site, leading to a reduction in the enzyme's catalytic activity. Unlike competitive inhibition, non-competitive inhibitors do not interfere with substrate binding at the active site. Instead, they bind either to the free enzyme or the enzyme-substrate complex, inducing conformational changes that lower the enzyme's ability to convert substrates into products. This form of inhibition affects the enzyme's efficiency without altering substrate affinity, making it distinct from competitive inhibition. Non-competitive inhibition plays a significant role in regulating enzyme activity within biological systems and is crucial for fine-tuning metabolic pathways and maintaining cellular homeostasis.

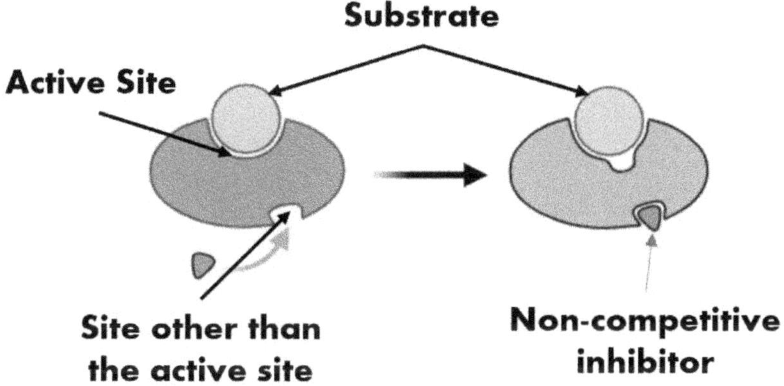

Figure 4 Mechanism of non-competitive inhibition

Non-competitive inhibition is characterized by an inhibitor binding to an allosteric site on the enzyme, a location distinct from the active site. This binding induces a conformational change in the enzyme, reducing its catalytic efficiency. Unlike competitive inhibitors, non-competitive inhibitors do not interfere with the substrate's ability to bind to the active site and can bind to either the free enzyme or the enzyme-substrate complex. As a result, increasing substrate concentration does not overcome non-competitive inhibition. In terms of enzyme kinetics, non-competitive inhibition reduces the maximum reaction velocity (V_{max}) without altering the Michaelis constant (K_m), reflecting that substrate binding remains unaffected while catalytic turnover is impaired. This can be visualized in a Lineweaver-Burk plot, where non-competitive inhibition increases both the x- and y-intercepts (Figure 5).

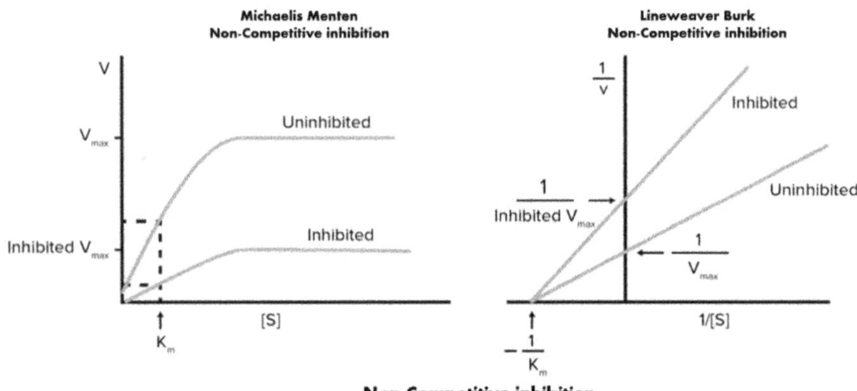

Figure 5 Effect of non-competitive inhibitors on the Michaelis-Menten curve and Lineweaver-Burk Plot

Despite being reversible, non-competitive inhibition is not overcome by higher substrate concentrations. It is also a classic example of allosteric regulation, which allows cells to finely modulate enzyme activity in response to physiological changes. This form of inhibition has practical implications in drug design, where many pharmaceutical compounds act as non-competitive inhibitors, and in enzyme kinetics research for characterizing enzyme-substrate interactions. In biotechnological applications, non-competitive inhibition offers potential for controlling enzymatic processes in industrial settings.

11.1.1.3 Uncompetitive Inhibition:

Uncompetitive inhibition (Figure 6) is a distinct form of enzyme inhibition where the inhibitor binds exclusively to the enzyme-substrate complex, rather than to the free enzyme. This type of inhibition occurs when an inhibitor molecule binds to the enzyme only after the substrate has been bound, forming an enzyme-substrate-inhibitor (ESI) complex. Unlike other types of inhibition, such as competitive or non-competitive inhibition, uncompetitive inhibition does not compete with the substrate for the enzyme's active site but rather interacts with the enzyme-substrate complex.

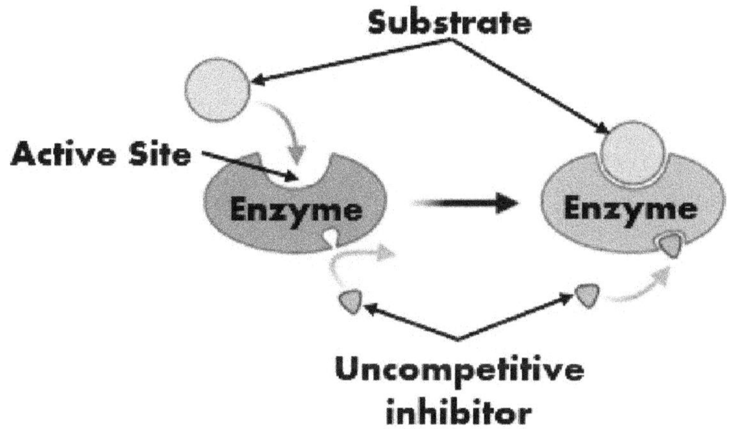

Figure 6 Mechanism of uncompetitive inhibition

In uncompetitive inhibition, the binding of the inhibitor to the enzyme-substrate complex results in a reduction of enzyme activity by preventing the conversion of the substrate into the product. This inhibition is characterized by a decrease in both the maximum rate of reaction (V_{max}) and the Michaelis constant (K_m), which is the substrate concentration at which the reaction rate is half of V_{max}. The effect on Km is particularly noteworthy because it reflects a change in the apparent affinity of the enzyme for the substrate. As the inhibitor binds to the enzyme-substrate complex, it effectively reduces the number of enzyme-substrate complexes available for the reaction, leading to a lower V_{max}. However, because the inhibitor does not prevent substrate binding but rather alters the enzyme-substrate complex, the K_m decreases proportionally, indicating that the substrate binds more tightly to the enzyme in the presence of the inhibitor (Figure 7).

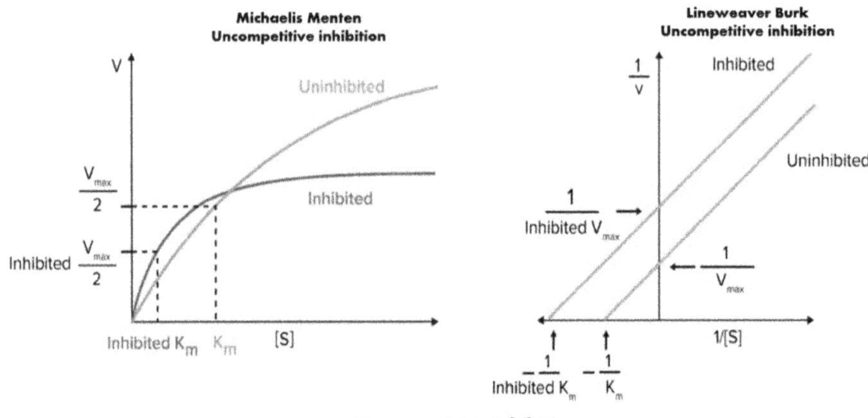

Figure 7 Effect of uncompetitive inhibitors on the Michaelis-Menten curve and Lineweaver-Burk Plot

A key feature of uncompetitive inhibition is that it is often observed in scenarios where the enzyme operates in a reaction mechanism involving a steady-state or pre-equilibrium formation of the enzyme-substrate complex. The inhibitor's binding is dependent on the presence of the substrate, and thus, the extent of inhibition can vary with substrate concentration. At higher substrate concentrations, the effect of the inhibitor becomes more pronounced because more enzyme-substrate complexes are available for the inhibitor to bind.

Overall, uncompetitive inhibition provides a unique insight into the regulation of enzyme activity and highlights the complex interplay between enzymes, substrates, and inhibitors. By understanding how uncompetitive inhibitors affect enzyme kinetics, researchers can gain valuable insights into enzyme mechanisms and develop targeted strategies for drug design and therapeutic interventions.

11.1.1.4 Mixed Inhibition

Mixed inhibition is a complex form of enzyme inhibition where the inhibitor can bind to both the free enzyme and the enzyme-substrate complex. This type of inhibition presents a more nuanced interaction between the enzyme, substrate, and inhibitor compared to other inhibition types, such as competitive or non-competitive inhibition. In mixed inhibition, the inhibitor's binding affects the enzyme's activity through multiple mechanisms, resulting in a combination of both competitive and non-competitive inhibition characteristics.

In mixed inhibition, the inhibitor can bind to the enzyme regardless of whether the substrate is present or not. When the inhibitor binds to the free enzyme, it reduces the enzyme's ability to bind to the substrate, which is characteristic of competitive inhibition. On the other hand, when the inhibitor binds to the enzyme-substrate complex, it prevents the conversion of the substrate into the product, akin to non-competitive inhibition. As a result, the mixed inhibitor affects both the enzyme's affinity for the substrate (K_m) and the maximum rate of the reaction (V_{max}).

The impact of mixed inhibition on enzyme kinetics is characterized by changes in both K_m and V_{max}. Specifically, the apparent K_m can either increase or decrease, depending on the relative affinities of the inhibitor for the free enzyme versus the enzyme-substrate complex. When the inhibitor binds more effectively to the enzyme-substrate complex, the K_m can decrease, reflecting an altered substrate binding affinity. Conversely, if the inhibitor binds preferentially to the free enzyme, the K_m increases, indicating reduced enzyme affinity for the substrate.

The effect on V_{max} is also notable. Mixed inhibition typically results in a decrease in V_{max}, which occurs because the inhibitor reduces the overall catalytic efficiency of the enzyme. This reduction in V_{max} is a combined result of the inhibitor's action on both the enzyme-substrate complex and the free enzyme. Unlike non-competitive inhibition, which affects V_{max} without altering K_m, mixed inhibition can change both parameters, making it a more intricate form of enzyme regulation.

Understanding mixed inhibition provides valuable insights into the dynamics of enzyme activity and regulation. It is particularly useful in drug development and enzyme engineering, where designing inhibitors that target specific enzyme states can lead to more effective therapeutic agents or enzyme modulators. By analysing the kinetics of mixed inhibition, researchers can better comprehend the interactions between enzymes and inhibitors, leading to more precise control over biochemical processes.

11.2 Irreversible Inhibition:

Irreversible inhibition involves the formation of a covalent bond between the inhibitor and the enzyme, leading to permanent or long-lasting inactivation of the enzyme's activity. Unlike reversible inhibition, where the inhibitor-enzyme complex can dissociate, irreversible inhibition results in a permanent modification of the enzyme's active site or another critical region, rendering the enzyme inactive. This type of inhibition cannot be reversed by changes in substrate concentration or environmental conditions. Irreversible inhibitors are often highly specific for their target enzymes and play a critical role in cellular processes, including the regulation of metabolic pathways. Because of their permanent effects, irreversible inhibitors are used in drug design, especially for targeting enzymes involved in disease progression, such as proteases or kinases. However, their strong specificity and lasting effects also mean that they must be carefully designed to avoid unwanted toxicity in therapeutic applications.

11.2.1 Features of Irreversible Inhibition:

11.2.1.1 Covalent Bond Formation:

Irreversible inhibitors typically react with functional groups on the enzyme, such as nucleophilic residues like cysteine, lysine, or serine, forming covalent bonds. This covalent modification causes permanent structural changes to the enzyme, effectively blocking its catalytic activity. By targeting specific amino acid side chains at the enzyme's active site or regulatory regions, irreversible inhibitors ensure that the enzyme can no longer bind to substrates or catalyse reactions. Because the inactivation is permanent, the enzyme remains non-functional even after the inhibitor is removed, requiring the synthesis of new enzyme molecules for activity to be restored. This mechanism of action makes irreversible inhibitors potent tools for enzyme-targeted therapeutics, though they must be used with caution due to their long-lasting effects.

11.2.1.2 Permanent Inactivation:

Once an irreversible inhibitor binds to the enzyme and forms a covalent bond, the enzyme's activity is permanently or for a long duration inhibited. The inhibitor-enzyme complex is highly stable and does not easily dissociate, resulting in a permanent or long-lasting loss of catalytic activity. The enzyme cannot regain its functionality without undergoing significant structural alterations or undergoing degradation and replacement. This irreversible binding ensures that the enzyme remains inactive until new enzyme molecules are synthesized, making irreversible inhibitors powerful tools in biochemical research and therapeutic applications.

11.2.1.3 Specificity:

Irreversible inhibitors are often highly specific for their target enzymes, as they typically bind to particular amino acid residues or active site features with precision. This high specificity allows for selective targeting of particular enzymes that play critical roles in disease processes or specific metabolic pathways. Such targeted inhibition can be advantageous in therapeutic contexts, where selective enzyme inhibition can mitigate unwanted side effects and enhance the efficacy of treatment by focusing on the precise enzymatic functions relevant to the disease.

11.2.2 Types of Irreversible Inhibition

There are several types of irreversible inhibition, each with distinct mechanisms of action:

11.2.2.1. Covalent Inhibition

Covalent inhibition involves the formation of a covalent bond between the inhibitor and the enzyme. This bond is typically formed between a functional group on the inhibitor and a reactive residue on the enzyme, such as a serine, cysteine, or lysine residue. Covalent inhibitors are often designed to mimic the substrate or transition state of the enzyme's reaction, allowing them to bind tightly and irreversibly. Examples of covalent inhibitors include:

- **Aspirin**: Aspirin acts as a covalent inhibitor of the enzyme cyclooxygenase (COX). It acetylates a serine residue in the active site of COX, thereby permanently inhibiting its ability to convert arachidonic acid into prostaglandins.
- **Penicillin**: Penicillin irreversibly inhibits bacterial transpeptidase enzymes by forming a covalent bond with a serine residue. This inhibition disrupts the synthesis of bacterial cell walls, leading to cell death.

11.2.2.2. Suicide Inhibition (Mechanism-Based Inhibition)

Suicide inhibition, also known as mechanism-based inhibition, occurs when the inhibitor is initially a non-reactive or minimally reactive molecule that becomes reactive only after undergoing a specific chemical transformation within the enzyme's active site. This transformation leads to the formation of a reactive species that covalently modifies the enzyme, leading to irreversible inhibition. The inhibitor essentially "commits suicide" by binding irreversibly to the enzyme. Examples include:

- **Allopurinol**: Allopurinol is used in the treatment of gout. It acts as a suicide inhibitor of xanthine oxidase, an enzyme involved in purine metabolism. Allopurinol is converted into an active form that covalently binds to xanthine oxidase, inhibiting its activity.
- **Clavulanic Acid**: Clavulanic acid is a suicide inhibitor of β-lactamase enzymes produced by bacteria. It irreversibly binds to the active site of the enzyme, preventing it from hydrolyzing β-lactam antibiotics.

11.2.2.3. Affinity Labelling

Affinity labelling involves the use of reactive compounds that specifically interact with certain residues in the enzyme's active site or other critical regions. These compounds are often analogs of substrates or transition states. Upon binding, they covalently modify specific amino acid residues, leading to irreversible inhibition. The specificity of affinity labeling allows for selective targeting of particular enzymes or enzyme classes. Examples include:

- **PMSF (Phenylmethylsulfonyl Fluoride)**: PMSF is an affinity label that irreversibly inhibits serine proteases by reacting with the active site serine residue. It is commonly used in biochemical research to study protease activity.
- **Iodoacetamide**: Iodoacetamide reacts specifically with cysteine residues in proteins, including enzymes. By covalently modifying these residues, iodoacetamide can irreversibly inhibit enzymatic activity, providing a tool for studying enzyme mechanisms and functions.

11.2.2.4. Reactive Substrate Analogues

Reactive substrate analogues are designed to closely resemble the enzyme's natural substrate but possess additional reactive groups that form covalent bonds with the enzyme. These analogues bind to the enzyme's active site and, through a chemical reaction, permanently modify the enzyme. Examples include:

- **Acetylcholine Esterase Inhibitors**: Some inhibitors of acetylcholine esterase, such as organophosphates, act as reactive substrate analogues. They covalently bind to the active site serine residue of the enzyme, leading to prolonged inhibition.

11.2.3 Examples of Irreversible Inhibitors:

Common examples of irreversible inhibitors include organophosphate compounds, such as nerve agents, which inhibit acetylcholinesterase and disrupt nerve signal transmission. Aspirin is another well-known irreversible inhibitor; it irreversibly inhibits cyclooxygenase enzymes (COX-1 and COX-2), thereby reducing inflammation and pain. Additionally, toxins like heavy metals, including mercury and lead, can act as irreversible inhibitors by binding covalently to critical enzyme residues, thereby disrupting various biochemical processes and causing cellular damage.

11.2.4 Practical Implications:

Irreversible inhibition has significant implications in both drug development and toxicology. In the realm of drug development, many therapeutics are designed as irreversible inhibitors to target specific enzymes involved in disease processes, offering long-lasting effects and potentially improved efficacy. For example, drugs like aspirin and certain cancer therapies are designed to provide sustained inhibition of their target enzymes, which can be beneficial for managing chronic conditions. Conversely, exposure to irreversible inhibitors, such as environmental toxins or industrial chemicals, can have detrimental effects on health. These substances can cause severe toxicity by permanently modifying essential enzymes, leading to disruptions in metabolic processes and adverse health consequences. Understanding the mechanisms and implications of irreversible inhibition is crucial for developing effective treatments and assessing the risks associated with toxic exposure.

11.2.5 Reversibility of Irreversible Inhibition:

In some instances, irreversible inhibition may exhibit reversible characteristics under specific conditions. For example, if the covalent bond between the inhibitor and the enzyme is relatively weak, it might undergo spontaneous hydrolysis or other chemical reactions over time. This can lead to partial or gradual restoration of enzyme activity. Despite this potential for partial recovery, the process is typically slow and may require substantial time before the enzyme's function is fully restored. Thus, while some degree of recovery might occur, irreversible inhibition generally results in prolonged or permanent inactivation of the enzyme.

CHAPTER XII

Feedback Inhibition

Feedback inhibition is a crucial regulatory mechanism in which the end product of a metabolic pathway binds as an allosteric inhibitor to an enzyme earlier in the same pathway, effectively modulating the pathway's flux. This form of negative feedback regulation serves as a control mechanism to maintain metabolic homeostasis by preventing the overproduction of metabolites. By binding to allosteric sites on key enzymes, the end product induces conformational changes that decrease the enzyme's catalytic activity, thereby slowing down or halting the production of additional metabolites. This regulation ensures that the cell's resources are used efficiently, and that the concentration of the end product remains within optimal levels. Feedback inhibition is a fundamental aspect of metabolic control, allowing cells to adapt dynamically to changing environmental conditions and metabolic demands, and preventing the wasteful accumulation of intermediates and products.

12.1 Features of Feedback Inhibition:

12.1.1 End Product Regulation:

Feedback inhibition occurs when the end product of a metabolic pathway inhibits an enzyme that acts earlier in the same pathway. As the concentration of the end product rises, it binds to a specific allosteric site on the enzyme, causing a conformational change that reduces the enzyme's catalytic activity. This prevents the further accumulation of the product and regulates the overall flow of the pathway. By controlling enzyme activity in response to the abundance of its end product, feedback inhibition ensures that metabolic processes remain balanced, conserving energy and resources, and preventing the unnecessary synthesis of excess metabolites. This regulatory mechanism (Figure 1) is vital for maintaining cellular efficiency and metabolic equilibrium in response to fluctuating environmental or physiological conditions. Table 1 shows that in each case, the product of the pathway often acts as an inhibitor, downregulating the enzyme's activity when concentrations become sufficient, thereby preventing overproduction. This is a classic example of feedback inhibition, where the accumulation of the end product inhibits the earlier steps of the pathway.

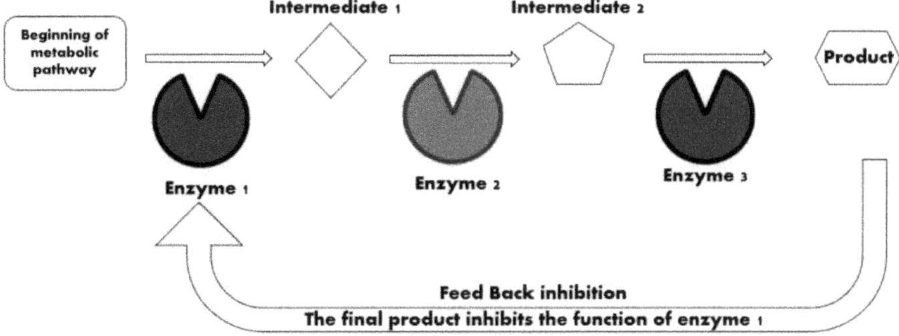

Figure 1 Mechanism of feedback inhibition

Table 1 Table illustrating examples of feedback inhibition, showing the enzyme, substrate, product, and the reaction they catalyse

Enzyme	Substrate	Product	Reaction Catalyzed
Threonine deaminase	L-Threonine	α-Ketobutyrate	Catalyses the conversion of L-threonine to α-ketobutyrate in the isoleucine biosynthesis pathway.
Aspartate transcarbamoylase	Carbamoyl phosphate	Carbamoyl aspartate	Catalyses the first step of pyrimidine biosynthesis, combining carbamoyl phosphate and aspartate.
3-Hydroxy-3-methylglutaryl-CoA reductase (HMG-CoA reductase)	HMG-CoA	Mevalonate	Catalyses the rate-limiting step in cholesterol biosynthesis, converting HMG-CoA to mevalonate.
Phosphofructokinase-1 (PFK-1)	Fructose-6-phosphate	Fructose-1,6-bisphosphate	Catalyses the phosphorylation of fructose-6-phosphate in glycolysis, producing fructose-1,6-bisphosphate.
Glutamine synthetase	Glutamate + Ammonia	Glutamine	Catalyses the ATP-dependent conversion of glutamate and ammonia to glutamine in nitrogen metabolism.
Pyruvate kinase	Phosphoenolpyruvate (PEP)	Pyruvate	Catalyses the final step in glycolysis, converting phosphoenolpyruvate to pyruvate.
Chorismate mutase	Chorismate	Prephenate	Catalyses the conversion of chorismate to prephenate in the biosynthesis of aromatic amino acids.
Adenylosuccinate synthetase	IMP (Inosine monophosphate)	Adenylosuccinate	Catalyses the conversion of IMP to adenylosuccinate in purine biosynthesis, a precursor to AMP.

12.1.2 Allosteric Inhibition:

The inhibition of the enzyme in feedback inhibition is mediated through allosteric regulation, where the binding of the end product to a regulatory site, distinct from the active site, induces conformational changes in the enzyme's structure. These conformational shifts result in decreased catalytic activity, effectively slowing or halting the enzymatic reaction. By preventing the enzyme from functioning efficiently, the pathway is regulated in a way that balances the production of end products with the cellular demand, ensuring metabolic efficiency and preventing the accumulation of unnecessary intermediates or products. This mechanism is key for maintaining homeostasis in complex biochemical pathways.

12.1.3 Negative Feedback:

Feedback inhibition is a classic example of a negative feedback mechanism, as it works to inhibit or reduce the activity of an enzyme, ultimately decreasing the flux through a metabolic pathway. By binding to an allosteric site on an enzyme early in the pathway, the end product effectively slows down the production process. This regulation is crucial for preventing the overaccumulation of excess end products, ensuring that resources are not wasted and maintaining the balance of metabolic processes within the cell. Through this mechanism, cells can fine-tune biochemical reactions in response to fluctuating metabolic needs.

12.1.4 Rapid Response:

Feedback inhibition offers a rapid and reversible mechanism for regulating metabolic pathways, responding swiftly to changes in the concentration of end products. As the levels of the end product increase, the inhibition is quickly triggered, reducing the activity of the enzymes involved in the pathway. This immediate response helps restore balance within the system, preventing the overproduction of metabolites and ensuring that resources are efficiently used. Once the levels of the end product decrease, the inhibition is lifted, allowing the pathway to resume its activity, maintaining homeostasis within the cell.

12.1.5 Fine-Tuning Metabolic Flux:

Feedback inhibition enables cells to precisely adjust the flux through metabolic pathways in response to shifting metabolic demands or environmental conditions. By regulating the activity of critical enzymes, this mechanism allows cells to control the rate at which metabolites are produced, ensuring that resources are utilized efficiently and only in the amounts needed. This dynamic regulation helps maintain cellular balance, optimizing the cell's ability to adapt to changes in its internal and external environment.

12.2 Example of Feedback Inhibition:

12.2.1 Biosynthesis Pathways:

Feedback inhibition is commonly observed in biosynthetic pathways involving multiple enzymatic steps for the synthesis of complex molecules. A classic example is the biosynthesis of the amino acid threonine, where the end product, threonine, acts as an allosteric inhibitor of the enzyme threonine deaminase. This enzyme catalyses the first step in threonine synthesis. As the concentration of threonine increases, it binds to threonine deaminase, inducing a conformational change that inhibits its activity. This feedback mechanism reduces the flux through the pathway, thereby preventing the overproduction of threonine and maintaining metabolic balance.

12.3 Role of feedback inhibition in biological system:

The role of feedback inhibition in biological systems is crucial for maintaining metabolic homeostasis, regulating cellular processes, and conserving energy resources. This fundamental mechanism allows cells to control the flux through metabolic pathways in response to changes in the concentration of end products. By modulating the activity of key enzymes, feedback inhibition ensures that metabolic pathways operate efficiently and only produce metabolites as needed, thus preventing the wasteful accumulation of excess products and optimizing resource use within the cell. It plays several key roles:

12.3.1 Metabolic Regulation:

Feedback inhibition regulates the activity of enzymes involved in metabolic pathways to ensure that metabolites are synthesized in appropriate quantities. When the levels of end products rise, feedback inhibition acts to inhibit key enzymes in the biosynthetic pathways, thereby preventing the overproduction of metabolites. This regulation helps maintain metabolic balance and ensures that resources are used efficiently, avoiding unnecessary accumulation of products and preserving cellular homeostasis.

12.3.2 Energy Conservation:

Feedback inhibition conserves energy resources by preventing the unnecessary consumption of substrates and energy precursors in metabolic pathways. By inhibiting the activity of key enzymes when end product levels are sufficient, cells avoid wasting energy on the synthesis of metabolites that are not immediately needed. This regulatory mechanism ensures that cellular energy and resources are utilized efficiently, maintaining optimal metabolic function and preventing the unnecessary expenditure of energy.

12.3.3 Prevention of Feedback Loop:

Feedback inhibition helps prevent feedback loops or runaway reactions in metabolic pathways. Without this regulatory mechanism, continuous production of end products could lead to excessive accumulation, which may disrupt cellular function or negatively impact other metabolic pathways. By ensuring that enzyme activity is modulated in response to end product levels, feedback inhibition maintains balanced metabolic processes and prevents the detrimental effects associated with the overproduction of metabolites.

12.3.4 Fine-Tuning Metabolic Flux:

Feedback inhibition allows cells to fine-tune the flux through metabolic pathways in response to changing metabolic demands or environmental conditions. By adjusting the activity of key enzymes according to fluctuations in end product levels, cells can optimize metabolic flux to meet cellular needs efficiently while minimizing waste. This dynamic regulation ensures that resources are allocated effectively, allowing cells to adapt to varying conditions and maintain metabolic balance.

12.3.5 Cellular Homeostasis:

Feedback inhibition contributes to maintaining cellular homeostasis by ensuring that metabolic pathways operate within appropriate limits. By regulating the synthesis of essential metabolites, feedback inhibition helps cells adapt to varying nutrient availability, metabolic stress, or environmental changes. This mechanism ensures that metabolic processes are finely tuned to current cellular needs, preventing imbalances that could disrupt cellular function and overall homeostasis.Top of Form

CHAPTER XIII

Nomenclature and Classification of Enzymes

13.1. Nomenclature

Enzymes are mostly named to give information about their functions rather than their structures. Nonetheless, the process of naming enzymes has three important characteristics, which are as follows: (i) Suffix: A substance that is identified by 'ase' as being an enzyme. It is noted that the names of the first enzymes learned are trypsin, chymotrypsin, and pepsin. (ii) Prefix: is recognized by the kind of reaction that the enzyme promotes such as hydrolase (hydrolysis reaction) and oxidase (oxidation reaction). (iii) Nature of the reaction: It is taken into account who the substrate is such as lactase (hydrolysis of lactose), Glucose oxidase (glucose oxidation), Urease (hydrolysis of urea).

13.2. Classification of Enzymes

Enzymes, the biological catalysts that facilitate biochemical reactions, are classified based on various criteria, including the type of reaction they catalyze, their structure, and the nature of their substrate. The classification system often employs a nomenclature that provides insights into their functions and characteristics.

13.2.1. Enzyme Commission (EC) Number: An EC number system for enzymes was created by the International Union of Biochemistry and Molecular Biology (IUBMB). Every enzyme's description begins with "EC" and is followed by four digits that indicate the hierarchy of enzymatic activity (extremely generic to very specific). In other words, the enzyme is categorized in general terms by the first number according to its mechanism, and then the remaining numbers add increasing specificity. An EC number is now used to name and identify enzymes in a systematic manner. This code, which consists of four levels of description, is used to categorize enzymes based on how they generally convert substrates into products. The enzyme classes based on the EC number and reaction type are mentioned in Table 1.

Table 1. Classification of enzymes based on EC number and type of reaction catalyzed

Class	Reaction catalysed
Oxidoreductases (EC 1)	Oxidation/reduction reactions
Transferases (EC2)	Transfer of a functional group from one substance to another.
Hydrolases (EC 3)	Formation of two products from a substrate by hydrolysis
Lyases (EC 4)	Non-hydrolytic addition or removal of groups from substrates. C-C, C-N, C-O or C-S bonds may be cleaved
Isomerases (EC5)	Intramolecular rearrangement, i.e. isomerization changes within a single molecule
Ligases (EC 6)	Join together two molecules by synthesis of new C-O, C-S, C-N or C-C bonds with simultaneous breakdown of ATP
Translocases (EC 7)	Catalyse the movement of ions or molecules across membranes or their separation within membranes

Every enzyme has a systematic name that indicates the reaction it catalyses as well as a four-part classification number. An EC number, for example, is four digits: a.b.c.d. Here "a" = class, "b" = subclass, "c" = sub-subclass and "d" = sub-sub-subclass. The reaction is described by the EC number's "b" and "c" parts, whereas "d" distinguishes between other enzymes that have similar functions based on the substrate that is actually used in the reaction. The NAD^+ oxidoreductase has an EC value of 1.1.1.1 for alcohol. The enzyme is known as ATP: D-hexose 6-phosphotransferase and its name suggests that it catalyses a phosphoryl group transfers from ATP to glucose. The EC number of this enzyme is 2.7.1.1. The 2 = class (transferase), 7 = subclass (phosphotransferase), 1 = a phosphotransferase that accepts hydroxyl groups, and 1 = acceptor of the phosphoryl group is D-glucose. A more common nomenclature for many enzymes in this case (hexokinase).

13.2.2. Based on Substrate Specificity: Enzymes are often named based on their substrate specificity or the type of molecule they act upon. Some important enzymes are mentioned in Table 2.

Table 2 Classification of enzymes based on substrate specificity

Enzyme	Catalysis of Reaction
Glucose oxidase	Glucose oxidation
Lactase	Hydrolysis of lactose
Lactate dehydrogenase	Eliminating hydrogen from lactate ion
Proteases	Break down proteins
Urease	Hydrolysis of urea
Lipases	Hydrolysis of lipids
DNA polymerases	DNA synthesis
Amylases	Breakdown of starch into sugars

13.2.3. Based on Structural Similarity: Enzymes can also be grouped based on similarities in their three-dimensional structures. Enzymes with similar structures and catalytic mechanisms might be categorized together, even if they catalyze different reactions or substrates (Table 3).

Table 3 Classification of Enzymes based on structural similarity

Enzyme Family	Representative Enzymes	Substrate	Type of Reaction Catalyzed	Structural Motif
Rossmann Fold Superfamily	Dehydrogenases (e.g., Lactate Dehydrogenase)	Lactate, NAD$^+$	Oxidation-reduction (redox reactions)	Rossmann fold (β-α-β)
	Kinases (e.g., Hexokinase)	Glucose, ATP	Phosphorylation	Rossmann fold (β-α-β)
	GTPases (e.g., Ras)	GTP	Hydrolysis of GTP to GDP	Rossmann fold (β-α-β)
TIM Barrel Superfamily	Enolase	2-phosphoglycerate	Lyase reaction (formation of phosphoenolpyruvate)	TIM barrel (α/β barrel)
	Aldolase (e.g., Fructose-bisphosphate aldolase)	Fructose 1,6-bisphosphate	Aldol cleavage (glycolytic pathway)	TIM barrel (α/β barrel)
Serine Protease Superfamily	Trypsin	Proteins (Peptide bonds)	Proteolysis (cleavage after Lys or Arg)	Serine protease fold
	Chymotrypsin	Proteins (Peptide bonds)	Proteolysis (cleavage after aromatic residues)	Serine protease fold
α/β Hydrolase Superfamily	Lipase	Triglycerides	Hydrolysis of ester bonds	α/β hydrolase fold
	Esterase	Esters	Hydrolysis of ester bonds	α/β hydrolase fold
Nucleotidyltransferase Superfamily	DNA Polymerase	DNA, dNTPs	DNA synthesis (nucleotide transfer)	Nucleotidyltransferase fold
	RNA Polymerase	RNA, NTPs	RNA synthesis (nucleotide transfer)	Nucleotidyltransferase fold
Glycoside Hydrolase Superfamily	Amylase	Starch, glycogen	Hydrolysis of α-1,4 glycosidic bonds	TIM barrel (α/β barrel)
	Cellulase	Cellulose	Hydrolysis of β-1,4 glycosidic bonds	TIM barrel (α/β barrel)
Oxidoreductase Superfamily	Cytochrome P450	Organic substrates, O$_2$	Oxidation (hydroxylation)	Cytochrome P450 fold
	Monooxygenases	Various substrates (e.g., fatty acids)	Oxygen incorporation into substrates	Cytochrome P450 fold

13.2.4.Based on Coenzyme or Cofactor Dependency: Enzymes often require non-protein components like coenzymes or metal ions for their catalytic activity. Enzymes that rely on similar coenzymes or cofactors may be grouped. Some of the examples based on this type of classification are given in Table 4

Table 4 Classification of enzymes based on coenzyme or cofactor dependency

Enzyme	Coenzyme/Cofactor	Substrate	Type of Reaction Catalyzed
Lactate Dehydrogenase	NAD⁺ (Coenzyme)	Pyruvate, NAD⁺	Redox (Conversion of pyruvate to lactate)
Glucose-6-Phosphate Dehydrogenase	NADP⁺ (Coenzyme)	Glucose-6-phosphate, NADP⁺	Redox (Oxidation of glucose-6-phosphate)
Succinate Dehydrogenase	FAD (Coenzyme)	Succinate	Redox (Oxidation of succinate to fumarate)
Pyruvate Carboxylase	Biotin (Coenzyme)	Pyruvate, CO_2	Carboxylation (Pyruvate to oxaloacetate)
Thymidylate Synthase	Tetrahydrofolate (Coenzyme)	dUMP, methylene-THF	Methylation (dUMP to dTMP)
Acetyl-CoA Carboxylase	Coenzyme A (Coenzyme)	Acetyl-CoA, CO_2	Carboxylation (Acetyl-CoA to malonyl-CoA)
Alanine Aminotransferase	Pyridoxal Phosphate (PLP, Coenzyme)	Alanine, α-ketoglutarate	Transamination (Alanine to pyruvate)
Carbonic Anhydrase	Zinc (Cofactor)	CO_2, H_2O	Hydration (CO_2 to bicarbonate)
Cytochrome c Oxidase	Copper (Cofactor)	Oxygen, electrons	Redox (Reduction of oxygen to water)
Hexokinase	Magnesium (Cofactor)	Glucose, ATP	Phosphorylation (Glucose to glucose-6-phosphate)
Superoxide Dismutase (Mn-SOD)	Manganese (Cofactor)	Superoxide radicals	Dismutation (Superoxide to oxygen and hydrogen peroxide)
Aconitase	Iron-sulfur cluster (Cofactor)	Citrate	Isomerization (Citrate to isocitrate)
Alcohol Dehydrogenase	NAD⁺ (Coenzyme)	Ethanol, NAD⁺	Redox (Ethanol to acetaldehyde)
Arginase	Manganese (Cofactor)	Arginine	Hydrolysis (Arginine to urea and ornithine)
Fatty Acid Synthase	Coenzyme A (Coenzyme)	Acetyl-CoA, Malonyl-CoA	Condensation (Fatty acid chain elongation)

Enzyme classification is crucial for organizing and understanding the vast array of enzymes found in biological systems. This classification system aids in predicting enzyme function, designing experiments, understanding metabolic pathways, and even engineering enzymes for various industrial or therapeutic applications. The diverse range of enzymes and their classifications reflects the intricacy and specificity of biological processes they govern.

CHAPTER XIV

Enzyme Classification Based on Reaction Type

14.1. Classification Based on Reaction Type:

Enzymes can be classified into six major classes based on the type of reaction they catalyse:

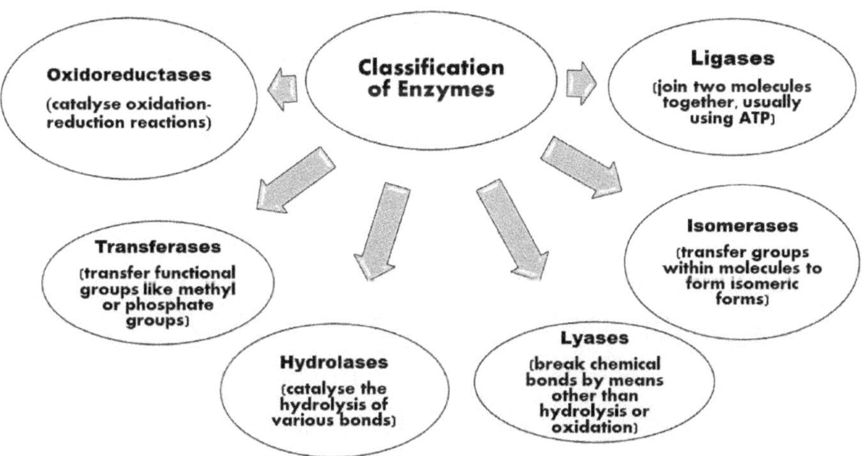

Figure 1 Classification of enzymes into six classes

14.1.1 Oxidoreductases:

Oxidoreductases are a class of enzymes that catalyze oxidation-reduction (redox) reactions, facilitating the transfer of electrons between molecules. In these reactions, electrons are transferred from a donor molecule, known as the reductant, to an acceptor molecule, called the oxidant. This electron exchange converts the substrates into their respective products. Oxidoreductases are critical in numerous biological processes, including cellular energy metabolism, biosynthetic pathways, detoxification, and intracellular signaling. They play key roles in processes like cellular respiration and photosynthesis, where they mediate redox reactions necessary for ATP production and energy transfer. These enzymes are also involved in maintaining redox balance within cells, making them vital for organismal homeostasis and defense mechanisms against oxidative stress.

14.1.1.1 Characteristics of Oxidoreductases

14.1.1.1.1 Catalysis of Redox Reactions

Oxidoreductases catalyze oxidation-reduction reactions by facilitating the transfer of electrons between two substrates. In these reactions, one substrate undergoes oxidation, losing electrons, while the other substrate is reduced by gaining those electrons. The enzyme acts as a mediator, ensuring the efficient transfer of electrons from the electron donor (the oxidized molecule) to the electron acceptor (the reduced molecule). This class of enzymes plays a pivotal role in maintaining cellular redox balance and is involved in various metabolic pathways that drive energy production and biosynthesis in living organisms.

14.1.1.1.2 Coenzyme or Cofactor Dependency

Many oxidoreductases require coenzymes or cofactors to facilitate electron transfer reactions. Coenzymes like NAD^+ (nicotinamide adenine dinucleotide) and FAD (flavin adenine dinucleotide) play a crucial role in these processes by serving as electron carriers. They shuttle electrons between the enzyme and the substrates, enabling the redox reactions to proceed efficiently. During the reaction, coenzymes accept electrons from the substrate being oxidized and then transfer them to the substrate being reduced. These coenzymes are essential for the proper functioning of oxidoreductases in key metabolic pathways such as cellular respiration, where they assist in the production of energy in the form of ATP.

14.1.1.1.3 Substrate Specificity

Oxidoreductases exhibit a high degree of specificity for their substrates, recognizing particular molecules that act as electron donors and acceptors in the redox reaction. The enzyme's active site is precisely structured to accommodate these specific substrates, ensuring efficient electron transfer. This substrate specificity is crucial for the enzyme's function in metabolic pathways, as it allows oxidoreductases to facilitate precise redox reactions in processes like energy production and biosynthesis. The ability of the enzyme to selectively bind its substrates ensures that redox reactions occur in a controlled and targeted manner within biological systems.

14.1.1.1.4 Classification of oxidoreductases:

Oxidoreductases are classified into various subclasses based on the specific types of oxidation-reduction reactions they catalyse (Table 1). Common subclasses include dehydrogenases, which facilitate the removal of hydrogen atoms from substrates; oxidases, which catalyze the transfer of electrons to oxygen molecules; peroxidases, which break down peroxides; and reductases, which catalyze the reduction of molecules by transferring electrons to them. Each subclass is specialized for distinct redox reactions, playing crucial roles in metabolic processes such as energy production, detoxification, and biosynthetic pathways, where electron transfer is vital.

Table 1 Classification of oxidoreductases based on reaction types

Subclass	Substrate	Function
Dehydrogenases	NADH, NADPH, FADH2 (as electron donors); various organic substrates like ethanol, lactate	Facilitate the removal of hydrogen atoms from substrates such as ethanol or lactate, playing key roles in energy production and metabolic pathways.
Oxidases	Oxygen	Catalyze the transfer of electrons to oxygen, resulting in the formation of water or hydrogen peroxide. Important in respiration and detoxification.
Peroxidases	Peroxides (e.g., hydrogen peroxide)	Break down peroxides by transferring electrons to them, helping in detoxification processes.
Reductases	NADH, NADPH (as electron donors); various organic substrates like ketones, aldehydes	Catalyze the reduction of molecules, such as converting ketones to alcohols or aldehydes to alcohols, involved in various biosynthetic and metabolic reactions.

14.1.1.1.5 Biological Functions:

Oxidoreductases play essential roles in a wide range of biological processes, including cellular respiration, photosynthesis, fatty acid metabolism, and the detoxification of reactive oxygen species (ROS). They are also involved in the biosynthesis of key molecules such as amino acids, lipids, and hormones. In cellular respiration, oxidoreductases facilitate the transfer of electrons in the electron transport chain, driving ATP production. In photosynthesis, they participate in light-dependent reactions to convert solar energy into chemical energy. Additionally, oxidoreductases help protect cells from oxidative damage by detoxifying harmful ROS, while also contributing to the synthesis of molecules necessary for growth, maintenance, and signaling within organisms.

14.1.1.1.6 Examples of Oxidoreductases:

14.1.1.1.6.1 Alcohol Dehydrogenase: Catalyses the conversion of alcohols to aldehydes or ketones, accompanied by the reduction of NAD^+ to NADH.

14.1.1.1.6.2 Cytochrome P450 Enzymes: Involved in the oxidation of various endogenous and exogenous compounds, including drugs, toxins, and xenobiotics, in the liver and other tissues.

14.1.1.1.6.3 Superoxide Dismutase: Catalyses the dismutation of superoxide radicals (O_2^-) into oxygen (O_2) and hydrogen peroxide (H_2O_2), protecting cells from oxidative damage.

14.1.1.1.6.4 NADH Dehydrogenase: Plays a key role in the electron transport chain of cellular respiration, transferring electrons from NADH to the respiratory chain for ATP production.

14.1.1.1.6.5 Glutathione Peroxidase: Catalyses the reduction of hydrogen peroxide (H_2O_2) and organic hydroperoxides using reduced glutathione (GSH) as a cofactor, protecting cells from oxidative stress.

14.1.2 Transferases:

Transferases are a class of enzymes that catalyse the transfer of functional groups, such as methyl, acyl, amino, or phosphate groups, from a donor molecule to an acceptor molecule. These enzymes are vital in various metabolic pathways, facilitating the movement of specific chemical groups between substrates. Transferases are essential in processes such as biosynthesis, where they aid in the formation of complex molecules, signal transduction for cellular communication, and cellular regulation by modifying proteins and other molecules. By mediating these group transfers, transferases play a pivotal role in maintaining cellular function and metabolic balance.

14.1.2.1 Characteristics of Transferases:

14.1.2.1.1 Functional Group Transfer:

Transferases catalyse the transfer of specific functional groups from a donor molecule to an acceptor molecule, facilitating the movement of various chemical moieties such as methyl, acyl, amino, phosphate, glycosyl, or sulfur groups. This group transfer is crucial in numerous biochemical processes, enabling the modification of molecules, regulating metabolic pathways, and supporting essential functions like DNA methylation, protein phosphorylation, and glycosylation. Through their ability to transfer diverse functional groups, transferases are integral to the dynamic regulation and synthesis of biological molecules.

14.1.2.1.2 Specificity:

Transferases exhibit a high degree of substrate specificity, recognizing particular donor and acceptor molecules that participate in the transfer reaction. The enzyme's active site is precisely structured to bind the specific chemical groups involved in the transfer process, ensuring efficient catalysis. This specificity allows transferases to carry out targeted biochemical modifications, such as the transfer of phosphate groups in phosphorylation reactions or amino groups in transamination, which are critical for cellular regulation, signal transduction, and metabolic processes. The precise recognition and accommodation of substrates enable transferases to perform their roles accurately within various biological systems.

14.1.2.1.3 Coenzyme or Cofactor Dependency:

Many transferases require coenzymes or cofactors to facilitate the transfer of functional groups between molecules. Coenzymes such as coenzyme A (CoA), adenosine triphosphate (ATP), and pyridoxal phosphate (PLP) act as carriers or cofactors, assisting in the transfer of specific chemical groups during the reaction. For instance, ATP often provides phosphate groups in phosphorylation reactions, while PLP plays a key role in transamination processes by transferring amino groups. These coenzymes and cofactors are essential for the proper functioning of transferases, enabling them to efficiently catalyze reactions that are vital for metabolism, biosynthesis, and cellular regulation.

14.1.2.2 Classification Based on Group Transferred:

Transferases are classified into various subclasses based on the type of functional group they transfer during reactions (Table 2). Common subclasses include kinases, which transfer phosphate groups; transaminases, responsible for transferring amino groups; acyltransferases, which facilitate the transfer of acyl groups; and methyltransferases, which transfer methyl groups. Each subclass is specialized for transferring a specific chemical group, playing key roles in different biological processes such as phosphorylation in signal transduction, amino group transfer in amino acid metabolism, and methylation in gene regulation. This classification helps in understanding the diverse functions of transferases in metabolism and cellular processes.

Table 2 List of transferases classified based on the type of functional group they transfer during reactions

Subclass	Substrate	Function
Kinases	ATP (phosphate donor)	Transfer phosphate groups to substrates, playing key roles in signal transduction and energy metabolism. Example: Hexokinase (transfers phosphate to glucose).
Transaminases	Amino acids (e.g., glutamate)	Transfer amino groups between amino acids and keto acids, crucial for amino acid metabolism and nitrogen metabolism. Example: Alanine transaminase (transfers amino groups between alanine and pyruvate).
Acyltransferases	Acyl groups (e.g., acetyl-CoA)	Transfer acyl groups to substrates, involved in lipid metabolism and biosynthesis. Example: Acetyl-CoA carboxylase (transfers acetyl groups to carboxylate acceptors).
Methyltransferases	Methyl groups (e.g., SAM)	Transfer methyl groups to substrates, important for gene regulation and protein modification. Example: DNA methyltransferase (adds methyl groups to DNA).

14.1.2.3 Biological Functions:

Transferases play diverse and critical roles in cellular metabolism, including regulating gene expression, facilitating signal transduction, and mediating post-translational modifications of proteins (Table 3). They are involved in the biosynthesis of essential biomolecules such as lipids, carbohydrates, and nucleic acids, ensuring proper cellular function and energy production. Additionally, transferases contribute to the detoxification of xenobiotics, helping to neutralize and eliminate foreign compounds from the body. By transferring specific functional groups between molecules, transferases are central to maintaining metabolic balance, cellular communication, and the synthesis of complex biomolecules essential for life.

Table 3 Examples of Transferases and the reaction catalysed by them

Transferase	Example	Reaction Catalysed
Kinases	Hexokinase	Catalyses the transfer of a phosphate group from ATP to glucose, forming glucose-6-phosphate in glycolysis.
	Protein Kinase A (PKA)	Phosphorylates target proteins at serine or threonine residues using ATP, regulating cellular signalling.
Transaminases	Aspartate Transaminase (AST)	Catalyses the transfer of an amino group from aspartate to α-ketoglutarate, forming oxaloacetate and glutamate.
	Alanine Transaminase (ALT)	Transfers an amino group from alanine to α-ketoglutarate, forming pyruvate and glutamate.
Acyltransferases	Carnitine Acyltransferase I	Transfers acyl groups from acyl-CoA to carnitine, facilitating the transport of fatty acids into mitochondria.
	Glycerol-3-phosphate Acyltransferase	Catalyses the transfer of fatty acyl groups to glycerol-3-phosphate, forming lysophosphatidic acid (lipid biosynthesis).
Methyltransferases	DNA Methyltransferase (DNMT)	Transfers a methyl group from S-adenosyl methionine (SAM) to cytosine residues in DNA, playing a role in gene regulation.
	Histone Methyltransferase (HMT)	Transfers methyl groups to histone proteins, influencing chromatin structure and gene expression.
Glycosyltransferases	UDP-glucose Glycogen Synthase	Catalyses the transfer of glucose from UDP-glucose to growing glycogen chains in glycogen synthesis.
Aminotransferases	Glutamate-Pyruvate Transaminase	Transfers an amino group from glutamate to pyruvate, forming alanine and α-ketoglutarate (amino acid metabolism).
Sulfotransferases	Tyrosine Protein Sulfotransferase	Catalyses the transfer of a sulphate group from PAPS (3'-phosphoadenosine-5'-phosphosulfate) to tyrosine residues on proteins.

14.1.3 Hydrolases:

Hydrolases are a class of enzymes that catalyze the hydrolysis of chemical bonds by adding water molecules, effectively breaking larger molecules into smaller components. These enzymes are crucial for various biological processes, including digestion, where they break down macromolecules like proteins, carbohydrates, and fats into their building blocks. Hydrolases also play key roles in metabolism, signal transduction, and intracellular trafficking by regulating the degradation of complex molecules and facilitating their conversion into usable forms. Their ability to cleave bonds makes hydrolases essential for maintaining cellular homeostasis and metabolic function.

14.1.3.1 Characteristics of Hydrolases:

14.1.3.1.1 Hydrolytic Activity:

Hydrolases catalyze hydrolysis reactions by adding water molecules to cleave chemical bonds between larger molecules. This process breaks the bond between two molecules, producing two smaller molecules as a result. The water molecule donates a hydroxyl group (OH^-) to one fragment and a hydrogen ion (H^+) to the other, effectively splitting the compound. This mechanism is essential for numerous biological processes, such as the breakdown of proteins, lipids, and nucleic acids into their basic components, enabling the body to utilize or recycle these smaller molecules in various metabolic pathways.

14.1.3.1.2 Substrate Specificity:

Hydrolases exhibit a high degree of substrate specificity, recognizing particular chemical bonds or functional groups within their substrate molecules that are targeted for hydrolysis. The enzyme's active site is precisely structured to bind the substrate, positioning it in a way that facilitates the addition of water and the subsequent breaking of the bond. This specificity ensures that hydrolases catalyze hydrolytic reactions efficiently and selectively, allowing them to carry out precise functions in processes like digestion, where different enzymes break down proteins, carbohydrates, and fats by targeting specific bonds within these macromolecules.

14.1.3.2 Classification Based on Substrate:

Hydrolases are classified into various subclasses based on the specific type of chemical bonds they hydrolyse (Table 4). Common subclasses include proteases, which hydrolyze peptide bonds in proteins; lipases, responsible for breaking ester bonds in lipids; nucleases, which hydrolyze phosphodiester bonds in nucleic acids; and glycosidases, which target glycosidic bonds in carbohydrates. Each subclass plays a distinct role in biological processes, such as protein degradation, fat metabolism, nucleic acid processing, and carbohydrate breakdown, highlighting the versatility and essential nature of hydrolases in maintaining cellular and metabolic functions.

Table 4 List of hydrolases classified into various subclasses based on the specific type of chemical bonds they hydrolyse

Subclass	Substrate	Function
Proteases	Peptide bonds in proteins	Hydrolyze peptide bonds, leading to protein degradation and turnover. Example: Trypsin (breaks down proteins into smaller peptides).
Lipases	Ester bonds in lipids	Hydrolyze ester bonds, facilitating the breakdown of lipids into fatty acids and glycerol. Example: Pancreatic lipase (digests dietary fats).
Nucleases	Phosphodiester bonds in nucleic acids	Hydrolyze phosphodiester bonds, leading to the breakdown of nucleic acids (DNA and RNA) into nucleotides or smaller fragments. Example: DNase (degrades DNA).
Glycosidases	Glycosidic bonds in carbohydrates	Hydrolyze glycosidic bonds, resulting in the breakdown of carbohydrates into simpler sugars. Example: Amylase (breaks down starch into maltose).

14.1.3.3 Cofactor Dependency:

Some hydrolases require cofactors or metal ions for their catalytic activity. These cofactors or metal ions, such as calcium, magnesium, or zinc, often function as essential components of the enzyme's active site, stabilizing the substrate or directly participating in the hydrolytic reaction. By facilitating the correct positioning of water molecules or stabilizing the transition state, these cofactors enhance the enzyme's ability to efficiently break chemical bonds. Their presence is critical for optimal enzymatic function, particularly in processes like digestion, DNA repair, and lipid metabolism, where precise bond cleavage is necessary.

14.1.3.4 Biological Functions:

Hydrolases play essential roles in a wide range of biological processes, including digestion, cellular metabolism, intracellular degradation, signal transduction, and the recycling of biomolecules. By breaking down complex molecules such as proteins, lipids, carbohydrates, and nucleic acids into smaller units, hydrolases enable cells to utilize these products for energy production, biosynthesis, or excretion. These enzymes are vital for maintaining cellular homeostasis, as they facilitate the degradation of macromolecules, allowing for the efficient recycling of cellular components and the regulation of various metabolic pathways.

14.1.4 Lyases:

Lyases are a class of enzymes that catalyze the cleavage or formation of chemical bonds in molecules without the addition or removal of water molecules, distinguishing them from hydrolases. These non-hydrolytic reactions involve the breaking or forming of bonds through mechanisms such as elimination, addition, or rearrangement. Lyases play crucial roles in various metabolic pathways, biosynthetic processes, and cellular signaling by facilitating the rearrangement of chemical bonds within substrates. Their actions are essential for processes such as the breakdown of complex molecules into simpler forms and the synthesis of new compounds, contributing to the regulation and maintenance of cellular functions.

14.1.4.1 Characteristics of Lyases:

14.1.4.1.1 Non-Hydrolytic Cleavage or Formation of Bonds:

Lyases catalyze the cleavage or formation of chemical bonds in molecules without the involvement of water molecules. Unlike hydrolases, which facilitate reactions by adding or removing water to break bonds, lyases operate through mechanisms that do not involve water. These enzymes either break bonds by mechanisms such as elimination, resulting in the formation of double bonds, or add groups to molecules to form new bonds. Their ability to catalyze such reactions is crucial for a variety of biological processes, including metabolic pathways and the synthesis of complex molecules.

14.1.4.1.2 Bond Cleavage or Formation:

Lyases can catalyze both the cleavage of single bonds and the formation of new double bonds, facilitating the rearrangement of molecular structures. Some lyases, known as lyases, are involved in breaking single bonds, while others, referred to as synthases, catalyze the formation of new double bonds. These reactions do not involve the addition or removal of water, unlike those catalyzed by hydrolases. By breaking existing bonds or creating new ones, lyases play a crucial role in various metabolic and biosynthetic processes, enabling the transformation and rearrangement of molecules necessary for cellular function and development.

14.1.4.1.3 Substrate Specificity:

Lyases exhibit specificity for their substrates by recognizing particular chemical bonds or functional groups that are involved in the cleavage or formation reactions. The active site of these enzymes is intricately structured to accommodate the substrate, ensuring that the bond-breaking or bond-forming processes occur efficiently. This specificity allows lyases to catalyze precise biochemical transformations, facilitating various metabolic and biosynthetic pathways by either breaking existing bonds or forming new ones without the involvement of water. Their tailored active sites enable them to carry out these reactions with high precision, impacting a wide range of cellular functions.

14.1.4.2 Classification Based on Reaction Type:

Lyases are classified into various subclasses based on the type of reaction they catalyse (Table 5). Common subclasses include carbon-carbon lyases, which catalyze the cleavage or formation of carbon-carbon bonds; carbon-oxygen lyases, responsible for the cleavage or formation of carbon-oxygen bonds; and carbon-nitrogen lyases, which facilitate reactions involving carbon-nitrogen bonds. Each subclass is specialized in catalyzing specific types of bond cleavage or formation, playing distinct roles in metabolic and biosynthetic pathways. This classification reflects the diverse range of chemical transformations lyases can perform, contributing to various cellular processes and biochemical reactions.

Table 5 List of lyases classified into subclasses based on the type of reaction they catalyse

Subclass	Substrate	Function
Carbon-Carbon Lyases	Carbon-carbon bonds	Catalyse the cleavage or formation of carbon-carbon bonds, leading to the breakdown or synthesis of carbon-based molecules. Example: Fumarase (catalyzes the conversion of fumarate to malate).
Carbon-Oxygen Lyases	Carbon-oxygen bonds	Catalyse the cleavage or formation of carbon-oxygen bonds, involved in reactions such as the decarboxylation or formation of carbon-oxygen bonds. Example: Decarboxylases (remove carboxyl groups from substrates).
Carbon-Nitrogen Lyases	Carbon-nitrogen bonds	Facilitate the cleavage or formation of carbon-nitrogen bonds, affecting processes like amino acid metabolism. Example: Amidases (catalyze the hydrolysis of amides to yield ammonia and the corresponding carboxylate).

14.1.4.3 Cofactor Dependency:

Some lyases require cofactors or metal ions for their catalytic activity. These cofactors or metal ions often serve as essential components of the enzyme's active site, aiding in the bond cleavage or formation process. By stabilizing the transition state or assisting in the proper positioning of substrates, cofactors and metal ions enhance the enzyme's ability to catalyze reactions efficiently. For example, certain lyases may utilize metal ions like magnesium or manganese to facilitate the catalytic process, ensuring effective transformation of substrates in metabolic and biosynthetic pathways.

14.1.4.4 Biological Functions of Lyases:

14.1.4.4.1 Metabolic Pathways:

Lyases participate in various metabolic pathways involved in the synthesis or breakdown of complex molecules. They are integral to key steps in carbohydrate metabolism, where they help in processes such as the breakdown of polysaccharides or the formation of new sugars. In amino acid metabolism, lyases facilitate the cleavage or formation of bonds within amino acids, impacting protein synthesis and degradation. Additionally, in lipid metabolism, lyases are involved in reactions that modify fatty acids and other lipid components. Their ability to catalyze these critical reactions underscores their importance in maintaining metabolic balance and enabling the efficient processing of biomolecules.

14.1.4.4.2 Biosynthetic Processes:

Lyases play a crucial role in biosynthetic processes that require the formation of new bonds or the rearrangement of molecular structures. They catalyze reactions in pathways leading to the synthesis of important biomolecules, including vitamins, cofactors, and secondary metabolites. By facilitating these key reactions, lyases contribute to the generation of essential compounds needed for various cellular functions and processes. Their ability to create or rearrange bonds is vital for the biosynthesis of molecules that support physiological functions and contribute to the overall metabolic network.

14.1.4.4.3 Cellular Signalling:

Some lyases play pivotal roles in cellular signaling pathways by catalyzing the formation or cleavage of signaling molecules. These enzymes are integral to regulating cellular responses to external stimuli, such as hormones or growth factors, and coordinating cellular activities in response to environmental changes. By modifying signaling molecules, lyases influence various cellular processes, including gene expression, metabolic adjustments, and cell growth. Their involvement ensures that cells can effectively interpret and respond to signals, maintaining homeostasis and adapting to fluctuating conditions.

14.1.4.4.4 Detoxification:

Lyases are involved in the detoxification of harmful substances by catalyzing reactions that convert toxic compounds into less harmful or more readily excretable forms. Through these reactions, lyases facilitate the transformation of potentially dangerous molecules into compounds that can be more easily processed or eliminated by the body. This detoxification process is crucial for maintaining cellular and systemic health, as it helps to mitigate the effects of environmental toxins, metabolic byproducts, and other harmful substances.

14.1.4.5 Examples of Lyases:

14.1.4.5.1 Decarboxylases: Catalyse the removal of carboxyl groups from substrates, resulting in the formation of new double bonds. Examples include pyruvate decarboxylase and amino acid decarboxylases involved in various metabolic pathways.

14.1.4.5.2 Dehydratases: Catalyse the removal of water molecules from substrates, leading to the formation of new double bonds or the rearrangement of molecular structures. Examples include fumarate hydratase and aldolase.

14.1.4.5.3 Synthases: Catalyse the formation of new bonds between substrates, resulting in the synthesis of larger molecules from smaller precursors. Examples include ATP synthase, which catalyzes the synthesis of ATP from ADP and inorganic phosphate.

14.1.5 Isomerases:

Isomerases are a class of enzymes that catalyze the rearrangement of atoms within a molecule, resulting in the conversion of one isomer into another. These enzymes are essential for various metabolic pathways, biosynthetic processes, and cellular regulation, as they facilitate the interconversion of isomeric forms of molecules. By enabling the transformation of molecules into their different structural forms, isomerases play a crucial role in optimizing biochemical reactions and maintaining metabolic balance, thereby supporting a wide range of physiological functions and processes.

14.1.5.1 Characteristics of Isomerases:

14.1.5.1.1 Isomerization Reactions:

Isomerases catalyze reactions that involve the rearrangement of atoms within a molecule, leading to the conversion of one isomeric form into another. These reactions do not involve the addition or removal of atoms but result in changes in the spatial arrangement or configuration of atoms within the molecule. By facilitating these structural changes, isomerases enable the interconversion of different isomers, which can be crucial for various biochemical processes and metabolic pathways. This capability allows cells to adapt to different needs and maintain biochemical balance.

14.1.5.1.2 Substrate Specificity:

Isomerases exhibit specificity for their substrates by recognizing particular molecular structures or functional groups that undergo rearrangement during the catalytic reaction. The active site of these enzymes is meticulously tailored to accommodate the substrate, ensuring efficient facilitation of the isomerization process. This specificity allows isomerases to precisely alter the spatial arrangement or configuration of atoms within the molecule, enabling the conversion of one isomeric form into another and playing a vital role in various metabolic and biosynthetic pathways.

14.1.5.1.3 Classification Based on Reaction Type:

Isomerases are classified into different subclasses based on the type of isomerization reaction they catalyse (Table 6). Common subclasses include racemases, which catalyze the interconversion of optical isomers; epimerases, which facilitate the interconversion of epimers; and cis-trans isomerases, which mediate the interconversion of cis and trans isomers. Each subclass plays a specific role in altering the molecular structure of substrates, contributing to various biochemical processes and metabolic pathways.

Table 6 List of isomerases classified into different subclasses based on the type of isomerization reaction

Subclasses	Substrate	Function
Racemases	Optical isomers	Catalyse the interconversion of optical isomers (enantiomers), affecting the spatial arrangement of atoms around a chiral center. Example: Alanine racemase (converts L-alanine to D-alanine).
Epimerases	Epimers	Facilitate the interconversion of epimers (stereoisomers that differ in configuration at only one chiral center). Example: UDP-glucose 4-epimerase (converts UDP-glucose to UDP-galactose).
Cis-Trans Isomerases	Cis and trans isomers	Mediate the interconversion of cis and trans isomers (isomers differing in the position of substituents around a double bond). Example: Peptidyl-prolyl cis-trans isomerase (catalyzes the isomerization of proline residues in peptides).

14.1.5.1.4 Cofactor Dependency:

Some isomerases require cofactors or metal ions for their catalytic activity. These cofactors or metal ions often act as essential components of the enzyme's active site, facilitating the isomerization reaction. By stabilizing the transition state or assisting in the proper alignment of substrates, cofactors and metal ions enhance the enzyme's ability to catalyse the rearrangement of atoms within the molecule, ensuring efficient conversion between different isomeric forms.

14.1.5.2 Biological Functions of Isomerases:

14.1.5.2.1 Metabolic Pathways:

Isomerases play essential roles in metabolic pathways involved in the interconversion of different forms of molecules. They catalyse critical reactions in carbohydrate metabolism, where they facilitate the rearrangement of sugar molecules, in amino acid metabolism, where they enable the transformation of amino acid isomers, and in lipid metabolism, where they assist in modifying fatty acid structures. By facilitating these transformations, isomerases help maintain metabolic balance and support various physiological functions essential for cellular health and energy production.

14.1.5.2.2 Biosynthetic Processes:

Isomerases are involved in biosynthetic processes that require the conversion of one isomeric form into another. They catalyse reactions in pathways leading to the synthesis of important biomolecules such as amino acids, nucleotides, and carbohydrates. By facilitating these conversions, isomerases ensure the proper formation of these essential compounds, supporting various cellular functions and contributing to overall metabolic processes.

14.1.5.2.3 Cellular Regulation:

Some isomerases are involved in cellular regulation and signaling pathways by catalysing reactions that generate signaling molecules or regulate enzyme activity. These enzymes play crucial roles in coordinating cellular responses to external stimuli and maintaining cellular homeostasis. By influencing the production or modification of signaling molecules, isomerases help modulate cellular activities and ensure that cells can adapt to changing conditions and respond effectively to various signals.

14.1.5.2.4 Detoxification:

Isomerases participate in detoxification processes by catalyzing reactions that convert toxic compounds into less harmful or more readily excretable forms. Through these transformations, isomerases aid in mitigating the effects of harmful substances, facilitating their removal from the body and helping to maintain cellular and systemic health.

14.1.5.3 Examples of Isomerases:

14.1.5.2.1 Hexokinase: Catalyses the conversion of glucose into glucose-6-phosphate, an essential step in glucose metabolism. This reaction involves the rearrangement of atoms within the glucose molecule.

14.1.5.2.2 Phosphoglucomutase: Catalyses the interconversion of glucose-1-phosphate and glucose-6-phosphate in glycogen metabolism. This reaction plays a key role in the synthesis and breakdown of glycogen.

14.1.5.2.3 Aldose-Ketose Isomerase: Catalyses the interconversion of aldose and ketose sugars by rearranging the carbonyl group within the molecule. This enzyme is involved in carbohydrate metabolism and sugar utilization pathways.

14.1.5.2.4 Cis-Trans Isomerase: Catalyses the interconversion of cis and trans isomers by rotating around a double bond within the molecule. This enzyme is involved in the biosynthesis of unsaturated fatty acids and the regulation of membrane fluidity.

14.1.6 Ligases:

Ligases, also known as synthetases or polymerases, are a class of enzymes that catalyze the joining (ligation) of two molecules, often coupled with the hydrolysis of high-energy bonds such as ATP. These enzymes are essential for various biological processes, including DNA replication, RNA transcription, protein synthesis, and metabolism. By facilitating the formation of new covalent bonds between substrates, ligases play a critical role in the synthesis and maintenance of complex biomolecules, enabling the accurate transmission of genetic information and the proper functioning of cellular processes.

14.1.6.1 Characteristics of Ligases:

14.1.6.1.1 Ligation Reactions: Ligases catalyze the formation of new covalent bonds between two molecules, resulting in the joining of the molecules into a single larger entity. These reactions typically require the input of energy, which is often derived from the hydrolysis of ATP or other high-energy phosphate donors. By providing the necessary energy for bond formation, ligases facilitate the synthesis of complex biomolecules and play a crucial role in processes such as DNA replication, protein synthesis, and metabolic pathways.

14.1.6.1.2 Substrate Specificity: Ligases exhibit specificity for their substrates, recognizing specific molecular structures or functional groups that undergo ligation during the catalytic reaction. The active site of the enzyme is intricately tailored to accommodate the substrates, facilitating the precise formation of new covalent bonds. This specificity ensures that ligases efficiently catalyze the joining of appropriate molecules, playing a vital role in various biological processes, including the assembly of complex macromolecules and the repair of cellular structures.

14.1.6.1.3 Cofactor Dependency: Many ligases require cofactors or coenzymes for their catalytic activity. These cofactors or coenzymes can serve as essential components of the enzyme's active site, providing additional chemical groups or assisting in the transfer of reaction intermediates during the ligation reaction. For example, ATP often acts as a coenzyme, supplying the energy necessary for the formation of covalent bonds. These auxiliary molecules are crucial for the efficient and accurate execution of ligase-catalyzed reactions, supporting a wide range of biological functions from DNA repair to metabolic processes.

14.1.6.1.4 Classification Based on Reaction Type: Ligases are classified into different subclasses based on the type of ligation reaction they catalyse (Table 7). Common subclasses include DNA ligases, which catalyze the joining of DNA strands; RNA ligases, which facilitate the joining of RNA strands; and aminoacyl-tRNA synthetases, which are responsible for attaching amino acids to tRNA molecules. Each subclass of ligase plays a specific role in critical biological processes, such as DNA replication, RNA processing, and protein synthesis, by ensuring the accurate assembly and modification of nucleic acids and proteins.

Table 7 List of ligases classified into different subclasses based on the type of ligation reaction

Subclass	Substrate	Function
DNA Ligases	DNA strands	Catalyse the joining of DNA strands by forming phosphodiester bonds, crucial for DNA replication and repair. Example: E. coli DNA ligase.
RNA Ligases	RNA strands	Facilitate the joining of RNA strands during RNA processing, including splicing and circularization. Example: T4 RNA ligase.
Aminoacyl-tRNA Synthetases	tRNA molecules and amino acids	Catalyse the attachment of amino acids to their corresponding tRNA molecules, essential for accurate translation of genetic code into proteins. Example: Valyl-tRNA synthetase.

14.1.6.1.5 Biological Functions of Ligases:

14.1.6.1.5.1 DNA Replication: DNA ligases play essential roles in DNA replication by catalyzing the joining of Okazaki fragments on the lagging strand and sealing nicks in the phosphodiester backbone of newly synthesized DNA strands. This action is crucial for maintaining the integrity and continuity of the DNA molecule, ensuring that the genetic information is accurately copied and repaired. By facilitating the formation of covalent bonds between adjacent DNA fragments, DNA ligases help complete the replication process and maintain genomic stability.

14.1.6.1.5.2 DNA Repair: Ligases are involved in DNA repair mechanisms, such as base excision repair, nucleotide excision repair, and mismatch repair, by sealing DNA strand breaks and restoring the integrity of the DNA molecule. In these repair processes, ligases facilitate the final step of the repair pathway by covalently linking adjacent DNA fragments or repaired sections, thereby ensuring the continuity of the DNA strand and maintaining genomic stability. Their activity is crucial for correcting damage and mutations that can arise from environmental factors, replication errors, or cellular processes, thereby preserving the fidelity of the genetic information.

14.1.6.1.5.3 RNA Processing: RNA ligases participate in RNA processing pathways by catalyzing the joining of RNA fragments during splicing, RNA editing, and RNA circularization processes. These enzymes are essential for the maturation and regulation of RNA molecules. In splicing, RNA ligases join exons after the removal of introns, ensuring the correct formation of functional messenger RNA (mRNA). In RNA editing, they facilitate modifications to RNA sequences, which can impact gene expression and function. Additionally, RNA ligases play a role in RNA circularization, which is important for the stability and translation of certain RNA molecules.

14.1.6.1.5.4 Protein Synthesis: Aminoacyl-tRNA synthetases catalyze the attachment of amino acids to their corresponding tRNA molecules, a critical step in ensuring the accurate translation of the genetic code during protein synthesis. These enzymes are highly specific, recognizing both the amino acid and its corresponding tRNA, and they catalyze the formation of an aminoacyl-tRNA complex. This complex delivers the correct amino acid to the ribosome during translation, allowing the ribosome to assemble proteins according to the genetic instructions encoded in mRNA. The high fidelity of aminoacyl-tRNA synthetases is essential for maintaining the accuracy of protein synthesis and overall cellular function.

14.1.6.1.5.5 Metabolic Pathways: Ligases play pivotal roles in various metabolic pathways by catalyzing the formation of covalent bonds between substrates. For example, in protein synthesis, ligases facilitate the formation of peptide bonds between amino acids, linking them into polypeptide chains. Additionally, in the citric acid cycle, ligases are involved in the synthesis of ATP, which is crucial for providing energy to drive numerous biochemical reactions. By enabling these critical bond-forming processes, ligases contribute significantly to cellular metabolism, energy production, and overall biochemical homeostasis.

CHAPTER XV

Coenzymes and Cofactors

Enzymes, as biological catalysts, often require additional non-protein molecules to carry out their catalytic functions efficiently. These molecules, known as cofactors and coenzymes, play crucial roles in enzyme activity by assisting in various aspects of the enzymatic process. They can participate directly in the chemical reactions, stabilize intermediates, or facilitate the binding of substrates. The classification of these essential molecules into two broad categories—cofactors and coenzymes—helps in understanding their diverse functions and contributions to enzymatic reactions.

15.1 Cofactors

Cofactors are typically inorganic ions or metal ions that are required for the proper functioning of certain enzymes. They often stabilize enzyme structures or reaction intermediates and are critical for enzyme activity. Examples of cofactors include metal ions such as zinc (Zn^{2+}), magnesium (Mg^{2+}), and iron (Fe^{2+}). Cofactors can be classified further based on their role in enzyme function:

15.1.1 Inorganic Cofactors: Metal Ions

Inorganic cofactors are essential non-protein components required by many enzymes to perform their catalytic functions effectively. Among these cofactors, metal ions such as zinc (Zn^{2+}), magnesium (Mg^{2+}), and iron (Fe^{2+}) play critical roles in stabilizing substrates, facilitating enzyme-substrate interactions, and participating directly in catalytic processes. These metal ions often bind tightly to the enzyme's active site, enabling or enhancing the enzyme's ability to catalyze specific biochemical reactions.

15.1.1.1 Zinc (Zn^{2+})

Zinc is a crucial metal cofactor required by many enzymes, including **carbonic anhydrase**. Carbonic anhydrase catalyses the reversible hydration of carbon dioxide (CO_2) to bicarbonate (HCO_3^-), a reaction vital for maintaining pH balance and facilitating CO_2 transport in the blood. Zinc ions help to stabilize reaction intermediates and polarize water molecules, making it easier for the enzyme to transfer protons during the reaction. Beyond carbonic anhydrase, zinc also plays a structural and catalytic role in enzymes like carboxypeptidase and alcohol dehydrogenase, where it assists in hydrolysis and oxidation-reduction reactions. In these cases, zinc acts as a Lewis acid, stabilizing negatively charged intermediates and facilitating nucleophilic attacks, crucial for catalysis.

15.1.1.2 Magnesium (Mg^{2+})

Magnesium ions are indispensable cofactors for a broad range of enzymes, particularly those involved in processes related to **nucleic acid metabolism**. For example, **DNA polymerase**, which is responsible for synthesizing new DNA strands during replication, requires magnesium to stabilize the negative charges on the phosphate backbone of nucleic acids. Magnesium ions assist in the correct positioning of nucleotide substrates and catalyse the formation of phosphodiester bonds. Additionally, enzymes such as kinases, which transfer phosphate groups from ATP to other molecules, rely on magnesium to stabilize the ATP molecule, ensuring proper alignment for phosphoryl transfer. The ubiquitous presence of magnesium in ATP-dependent reactions underlines its essential role in cellular metabolism and energy transfer.

15.1.1.3 Iron (Fe^{2+}/Fe^{3+})

Iron is another critical inorganic cofactor, particularly involved in **redox reactions** where electron transfer is required. Iron ions can exist in two oxidation states, Fe^{2+} (ferrous) and Fe^{3+} (ferric), allowing them to easily accept and donate electrons during biochemical reactions. This property is exploited by enzymes such as **cytochromes** and **peroxidases**. Cytochromes, particularly those in the electron transport chain, utilize iron in haeme groups to transfer electrons between different protein complexes, ultimately contributing to the production of ATP in oxidative phosphorylation. Similarly, peroxidases use iron to catalyse the reduction of hydrogen peroxide (H_2O_2) into water, a critical detoxification reaction in cells. The iron-dependent enzymes' ability to catalyse redox reactions highlights their importance in metabolic processes, respiration, and cellular defense mechanisms.

Other inorganic cofactors that are involved in various enzymatic activities are given in Table 1

Table 1 Summary of metal ion cofactors, enzymes, and function of these enzymes

Cofactors	Enzyme	Function of enzyme
Zinc (Zn^{2+})	Alcohol dehydrogenase	Responsible for reducing nicotinamide adenine dinucleotide (NAD^+) to NADH, which allows alcohols to be interconverted with aldehydes or ketones
	Carbonic anhydrase	The bidirectional conversion of carbon dioxide (CO_2) and water (H_2O) into bicarbonate (HCO_3^-) and protons (H^+) is catalysed by carbonic anhydrases (CAs).
	DNA polymerase	DNA polymerization
Ferrous (Fe^{2+}) or Ferric (Fe^{3+})	Catalase	Breaks down hydrogen peroxide into oxygen and water
	Cytochrome (via Heme)	In the electron transport chain, cytochrome c moves one electron at a time from the third complex—cytochrome bc1—to the fourth complex—cytochrome c oxidase—via its heme group.
	Nitrogenase	Nitrogen from the atmosphere (N_2) is transformed into nitrogen that plants and other organisms can use, ammonia (NH_3). Two key proteins are usually the main constituents: the molybdenum-iron protein (MoFe protein) and the iron protein (Fe protein).
	Hydrogenase	An enzyme called a hydrogenase is responsible for the reversible oxidation of molecular hydrogen. (FeFe)-hydrogenase, (Ni-Fe)-hydrogenase, and (Fe)-hydrogenase are the three major forms of hydrogenase.
Magnesium (Mg^{2+})	Glucose 6-phosphatase	Glucose 6-phosphatase's principal function is to catalyse the last stage of glycogenolysis and gluconeogenesis. It changes glucose 6-phosphate (G6P) into inorganic phosphate and glucose.
	Hexokinase	Hexokinase catalyzes the first step of glycolysis, the breakdown of glucose into pyruvate.
	DNA polymerase	DNA polymerization
Manganese (Mn^{2+})	Arginase	Contribute the urea cycle's conversion of arginine to ornithine and urea.
	Ribonucleotide reductase	Ribonucleotide-to-2'-deoxyribonucleotide converting enzyme, which produces the precursors required for DNA synthesis and repair
Nickel (Ni^{2+})	Urease	breakdown of urea into its component parts
Molybdenum (Mo)	Nitrate reductase	An enzyme that plays a role in nitrogen metabolism. The transformation of nitrate (NO_3^-) to nitrite (NO_2^-) is catalysed by nitrate reductase and is a crucial step in the uptake of nitrogen in plants and microbes.
	Nitrogenase	A key component of the biological nitrogen fixation process is the enzyme complex known as nitrogenase, which transforms atmospheric nitrogen (N_2) into ammonia (NH_3), a form of nitrogen required for the production of amino acids and other biomolecules. The two primary components are the Fe protein and the MoFe protein
	Xanthine oxidase	Involved in the purine metabolism pathway. It catalyses the production of uric acid from xanthine and hypoxanthine.
Cupric or copper (Cu^{2+})	Cytochrome oxidase	Serves as a cofactor for complex IV, also referred to as cytochrome c oxidase, an essential enzyme in the electron transport cycle of cellular respiration. Certain prokaryotes' plasma membranes and the inner mitochondrial membrane of eukaryotic cells both contain cytochrome c oxidase.
Potassium (K^+)	Pyruvate kinase	Controls cell metabolism by catalysing the conversion of phosphoenolpyruvate and ADP into pyruvate and ATP during glycolysis.

15.2 Coenzymes: Organic Molecules Facilitating Catalysis

Coenzymes are organic molecules that transiently bind to enzymes, playing a critical role in facilitating catalytic processes. Unlike prosthetic groups, which are permanently attached to enzymes, coenzymes associate with the enzyme only during the catalytic cycle and are often regenerated afterward for reuse. They assist in various biochemical reactions, particularly by acting as carriers for electrons, hydrogen atoms, or specific chemical groups. Some of the most important coenzymes include **Nicotinamide Adenine Dinucleotide (NAD$^+$)**, **Flavin Adenine Dinucleotide (FAD)**, and **Coenzyme A (CoA)**, each of which plays a specialized role in metabolism.

15.2.1 Nicotinamide Adenine Dinucleotide (NAD$^+$)

NAD$^+$ is a key coenzyme involved in **redox reactions** across many metabolic pathways. It functions primarily as an electron carrier, alternating between its oxidised form (NAD$^+$) and its reduced form (NADH). During catabolic reactions, such as **glycolysis** and the **citric acid cycle**, NAD$^+$ accepts electrons (in the form of hydride ions, H$^-$) from substrates, converting into NADH. This reduction step allows NAD$^+$ to serve as an electron acceptor, helping to oxidise substrates in metabolic pathways. NADH, in turn, donates these electrons to the electron transport chain, ultimately driving the production of ATP during oxidative phosphorylation. NAD$^+$ plays a crucial role in cellular respiration, providing the necessary electron shuttling for energy production. Its ability to cycle between oxidized and reduced states makes it essential for maintaining redox balance in the cell.

15.2.2 Flavin Adenine Dinucleotide (FAD)

FAD is another important coenzyme that functions in **redox reactions**. Similar to NAD$^+$, FAD participates in the transfer of electrons and protons, but it often catalyses reactions where more complex oxidation steps occur. FAD accepts two electrons and two protons to form **FADH$_2$**, its reduced form. This electron transfer is critical in processes such as the **Krebs cycle**, particularly in the oxidation of succinate to fumarate by **succinate dehydrogenase**. FADH$_2$, like NADH, donates its electrons to the electron transport chain, but it contributes them to a different complex (Complex II), resulting in slightly lower ATP yield compared to NADH. Despite this, FAD's involvement in oxidative metabolism is essential for efficient energy production.

15.2.3 Coenzyme A (CoA)

Coenzyme A is a versatile coenzyme involved in the transfer of **acyl groups**. Its most well-known role is in the **Krebs cycle**, where it carries acetyl groups derived from pyruvate into the cycle as **acetyl-CoA**. The acetyl group is transferred to oxaloacetate to form citrate, which is the first step of the Krebs cycle. CoA is involved in numerous other metabolic processes, including **fatty acid oxidation**, where it helps transfer fatty acids for breakdown into acetyl-CoA. This acyl group transfer ability of CoA is critical for the metabolism of carbohydrates, fats, and proteins, making it a central player in cellular energy balance and biosynthetic pathways. The reactive thiol group (-SH) of CoA allows it to form high-energy thioester bonds with acyl groups, facilitating their transfer between different enzymes.

15.3 Prosthetic Groups: Essential and Permanently Bound Enzyme Components

Prosthetic groups are non-protein components that are tightly or permanently bound to enzymes and are essential for their catalytic activity. Unlike coenzymes, which transiently associate with enzymes, prosthetic groups remain attached throughout the enzyme's lifecycle, often through covalent bonds. These groups play critical roles in the enzyme's function by stabilizing reaction intermediates or directly participating in the reaction mechanism. Two prominent examples of prosthetic groups are **haeme** and **biotin**, which are vital for oxygen binding and carboxylation reactions, respectively.

15.3.1 Haeme

Haeme is a well-known prosthetic group, most famously found in oxygen-binding proteins such as **haemoglobin** and **myoglobin**, as well as in a variety of enzymes like **cytochromes**. Structurally, haeme consists of an iron ion (Fe^{2+}) bound within a porphyrin ring. In **haemoglobin** and **myoglobin**, haeme is crucial for binding and transporting oxygen. In hemoglobin, found in red blood cells, the iron ion in haeme binds oxygen in the lungs and releases it in tissues, facilitating oxygen transport throughout the body. Myoglobin, found in muscle tissue, binds oxygen with high affinity and stores it for muscle activity. The iron ion in haeme allows it to alternate between different oxidation states (Fe^{2+} and Fe^{3+}), which is crucial for its ability to bind and release oxygen molecules. Haeme is also involved in **cytochrome enzymes** in the electron transport chain, where it plays a role in electron transfer, driving cellular respiration and ATP production.

15.3.2 Biotin

Biotin, also known as **vitamin B7**, serves as a prosthetic group for enzymes involved in **carboxylation reactions**, such as **pyruvate carboxylase** and **acetyl-CoA carboxylase**. Biotin is covalently attached to the enzyme through an amide linkage to a lysine residue, ensuring it remains tightly bound during catalysis. In its role as a prosthetic group, biotin facilitates the transfer of carbon dioxide (CO_2) to substrates, enabling carboxylation. For example, in pyruvate carboxylase, biotin carries CO_2 and transfers it to pyruvate, converting it to oxaloacetate, an essential intermediate in gluconeogenesis. Biotin's ability to form a covalent bond with CO_2 is vital for this process, making it indispensable in metabolic pathways that synthesize glucose and fatty acids.

15.4 Vitamins and derivatives used as enzyme cofactors

Although the body cannot synthesise these vitamins and their derivatives at sufficient levels, it is vital to remember that they must be received through the diet for various biochemical activities. Ensuring an adequate intake of these vitamins to maintain general health and good enzymatic activity requires a varied and balanced diet. Cofactors or coenzymes for enzymes are frequently provided by vitamins and their derivatives. Non-protein substances called cofactors help enzymes do their functions. The following is a list of vitamins and their derivatives that function as cofactors (Table 2).

Table 2 Examples of vitamins and derivatives used as a cofactor and activates

Vitamin	Example of cofactor containing Enzymes	Cofactor	Activities: Group(s) transferred
B1: Thiamine	Transketolase	Thiamine pyrophosphate	Aldehyde group, Decarboxylation
	Pyruvate dehydrogenase		
	α-ketoglutarate dehydrogenase		
B2: Riboflavin	oxidoreductases	FMN	Electrons
	Cytochrome-b5 reductase	FAD	
	Methylene tetrahydrofolate reductase		
B3: Niacin	Glyceraldehyde 3-phosphate dehydrogenase	NAD+	
	Isocitrate dehydrogenase (IDH) (dual coenzyme specificity)	NAD^+ and $NADP^+$	
	Transhydrogenase	$NADP^+$	
B5: Pantothenic acid	Acetyl-CoA synthetase	Coenzyme A	Acetyl group and other acyl groups
B6: Pyridoxine	Aromatic amino acid decarboxylases	Pyridoxal phosphate	Amino and carboxyl groups
	Alanine aminotransferase		
B9: Folic acid	Serine hydroxyl methyl transferase	Tetrahydrofolic acid	Methyl, formyl, methylene and form imino groups
	Thymidylate synthase		
Vitamin B12	Methionine synthase	Methylcobalamin	acyl groups
B12: Cobalamine	Methylmalonyl-CoA mutase	Cobalamine	hydrogen, alkyl groups
B7: Biotin	Pyruvate carboxylase	Biotin	CO2
	Acetyl-CoA carboxylase		
Vitamin K	NADH dehydrogenase	Menaquinone	Carbonyl group and electrons
Vitamin C	Prolyl hydroxylase	Ascorbic acid	Electrons

15.5 Functions of Cofactors and Coenzymes

The primary functions of cofactors and coenzymes in enzymatic reactions can be summarized as follows:

15.5.1 Catalytic Assistance: Cofactors and coenzymes can assist in the catalytic process by stabilizing reaction intermediates or by participating directly in chemical transformations. For example, magnesium ions stabilize negative charges on the substrate in kinases, while NAD^+ participates in redox reactions by accepting electrons.

15.5.2 Substrate Binding: They can help in the correct binding of substrates to the enzyme's active site. This is seen with coenzymes like CoA, which helps in the transfer of acyl groups, thereby facilitating substrate recognition and catalysis.

15.5.3 Structural Stabilization: Cofactors like metal ions contribute to the structural integrity of the enzyme, ensuring that it maintains its functional conformation. For instance, zinc ions are crucial for the structural stabilization of many enzymes.

15.5.4 Regulation of Enzyme Activity: Some cofactors and coenzymes play roles in the regulation of enzyme activity by modifying the enzyme's affinity for its substrate or by influencing the enzyme's catalytic efficiency.

Understanding cofactors and coenzymes is essential for elucidating the mechanisms of enzymatic reactions and for applying this knowledge in fields such as biochemistry, medicine, and biotechnology. By studying these non-protein molecules, scientists can gain insights into enzyme function, design targeted inhibitors, and develop therapeutic strategies for diseases linked to enzymatic deficiencies. The diverse roles of cofactors and coenzymes underscore their significance in maintaining the dynamic and efficient operation of biological systems.

CHAPTER XVI

Determination of Enzyme Structure

The determination of enzyme structure is a fundamental aspect of biochemical research, critical to understanding the intricate mechanisms that govern enzyme function, regulation, and interactions. Enzymes, as highly specialized biological catalysts, rely on their three-dimensional (3D) structures to bind substrates, facilitate chemical reactions, and ensure specificity and efficiency. By elucidating the structural features of enzymes, scientists can gain insights into how enzymes catalyse reactions, how they are regulated, and how their activity can be modulated for various applications. Structural determination also plays a vital role in rational drug design, enzyme engineering, and the development of biocatalysts for industrial processes.

The methods employed to determine enzyme structures have evolved significantly, with techniques such as X-ray crystallography, nuclear magnetic resonance (NMR) spectroscopy, cryo-electron microscopy (cryo-EM), and computational modelling leading the way. X-ray crystallography has long been the gold standard for resolving atomic-level details of enzyme structures, providing precise information about the active site and substrate binding regions. NMR spectroscopy and cryo-EM offer complementary techniques, especially for enzymes that are difficult to crystallize or are part of larger complexes. In recent years, advances in computational tools, including molecular dynamics simulations and artificial intelligence-based approaches, have further expanded the possibilities for modelling enzyme structures and predicting their dynamic behaviour.

The determination of enzyme structure is not just an academic pursuit but a crucial step in practical applications, ranging from the development of targeted therapies in medicine to the optimization of enzyme-based industrial processes. By understanding the detailed structure of enzymes, researchers can design inhibitors or activators, optimize enzyme performance under specific conditions, and engineer novel enzymes for a wide array of biotechnological applications. This chapter will explore the various methods of enzyme structure determination, their applications, and their significance in advancing the understanding of enzymatic function and the development of new technologies.

16.1 Determination of Primary Structure of Enzymes

The primary structure of an enzyme refers to the specific sequence of amino acids that make up its polypeptide chain. This sequence is crucial as it dictates the enzyme's higher-level structures—secondary, tertiary, and quaternary—which, in turn, determine its functional properties. Determining the primary structure is essential for understanding an enzyme's function, stability, and interaction with substrates and inhibitors. The amino acid sequence of enzymes can be determined through various methods, including Edman degradation, mass spectrometry (MS), and DNA sequencing techniques. Edman degradation involves sequentially removing amino acids from the N-terminal end of a peptide and identifying them, while MS provides a more rapid and precise method of sequence determination by measuring the mass-to-charge ratio of peptide fragments. In recent years, advancements in genomics have enabled DNA sequencing to predict an enzyme's amino acid sequence based on its corresponding gene, further enhancing our ability to determine primary structures. Understanding the primary structure is foundational for further analysis of enzyme function, engineering, and application in biotechnological and pharmaceutical industries. The primary structure of the enzyme is determined by amino acid sequencing using different methods such as

16.1.1 Edman Degradation:

Edman Degradation is a biochemical technique used to determine the amino acid sequence in a peptide or protein. It was developed by Pehr Edman in 1950. The process involves selectively removing the N-terminal amino acid residue from the peptide chain, which is then identified and analysed. The steps of Edman degradation sequencing are depicted in Figure 1.

1. **Reaction**: The N-terminal amino acid of the peptide is reacted with phenylisothiocyanate (PITC) under mildly alkaline conditions. This forms a cyclic phenylthiocarbamoyl derivative of the N-terminal amino acid.

2. **Cleavage**: The cyclic derivative is then treated with a mildly acidic reagent, typically trifluoroacetic acid (TFA). This cleaves the N-terminal amino acid from the rest of the peptide chain, leaving the other amino acids intact.

3. **Identification**: The cleaved N-terminal amino acid can be identified using techniques such as chromatography or mass spectrometry.

4. **Repetition**: The process can be repeated to sequentially identify each subsequent amino acid in the peptide chain, one at a time.

This sequential process allows for the determination of the complete amino acid sequence of the peptide or protein. Edman Degradation has been widely used in biochemistry and protein sequencing, although it has limitations, particularly with larger proteins where repetitive degradation can lead to inaccuracies. More modern methods, such as mass spectrometry, have largely replaced it for large-scale protein sequencing.

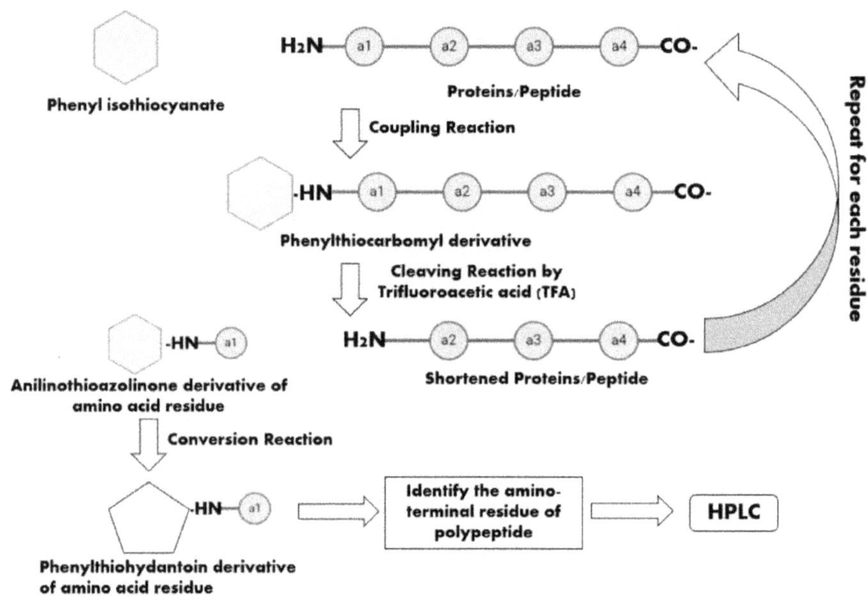

Figure 1 Edmand degradation scheme for determination of the amino acid sequence of polypeptide/proteins

16.1.2 Mass Spectrometry: Mass-to-charge ratios of peptide fragments can be measured using contemporary mass spectrometry techniques to offer fast and precise amino acid sequencing. Contemporary mass spectrometry techniques have revolutionized the field of proteomics, enabling rapid and precise amino acid sequencing of peptides. The steps involved in mass spectroscopy are as follows:

1. **Ionization**: Peptides are ionized using techniques like electrospray ionization (ESI) or matrix-assisted laser desorption/ionization (MALDI). This converts them into charged ions, making them suitable for mass analysis.

2. **Fragmentation**: Once ionized, peptides are subjected to fragmentation techniques such as collision-induced dissociation (CID) or electron transfer dissociation (ETD). This breaks them into smaller fragments while preserving the peptide's sequence-specific information.

3. **Mass Analysis**: The resulting peptide fragments are then analysed based on their mass-to-charge ratio (m/z) using a mass analyser. Modern mass analysers, like ion traps or time-of-flight (TOF) analysers, offer high resolution and accuracy in measuring m/z values.

4. **Data Interpretation**: The mass spectra obtained from the fragmentation are analysed using computational algorithms and databases. By comparing the observed fragment masses to theoretical masses of peptides derived from known protein sequences, the amino acid sequence of the peptide can be deduced.

5. **Database Searching**: Once the peptide sequence is obtained, it can be searched against protein sequence databases to identify the protein from which it originated.

This approach, known as tandem mass spectrometry (MS/MS), is highly sensitive and capable of sequencing peptides with high speed and accuracy. It's widely used in proteomics research for protein identification, characterization, and quantification, as well as for studying post-translational modifications and protein-protein interactions.

16.1.3 Sanger Sequencing (Automated Sequencing):

Sanger sequencing, also known as chain termination sequencing, is a widely used method for determining the nucleotide sequence of DNA. However, it can indeed be adapted for protein sequencing, although its primary application remains in DNA sequencing. Here's how it can be modified for protein sequencing:

1. **Conversion to DNA**: Since Sanger sequencing directly reads the sequence of DNA, protein sequencing requires converting the protein sequence into its corresponding DNA sequence. This is typically done by reverse-translating the protein sequence using the genetic code, which assigns specific codons (DNA triplets) to each amino acid.

2. **Synthesis of DNA Templates**: Once the protein sequence is converted into its DNA sequence, synthetic DNA templates representing the complementary sequence are generated. These templates serve as the substrates for the sequencing reaction.

3. **Sequencing Reaction**: The sequencing reaction follows the same principles as traditional Sanger sequencing for DNA. Fluorescently labelled nucleotides are incorporated into the growing DNA strand, and the termination of chain extension is detected based on fluorescence signals.

4. **Electrophoresis and Detection**: After the sequencing reaction, the DNA fragments are separated by size using capillary electrophoresis. The fluorescent signals from the terminating nucleotides are detected as the DNA fragments pass through a detection window.

5. **Data Analysis**: The fluorescent signals are recorded and analysed to determine the sequence of DNA bases, which corresponds to the amino acid sequence of the protein after reverse translation.

While Sanger sequencing can be adapted for protein sequencing, it's not as commonly used for this purpose compared to other techniques such as Edman degradation or mass spectrometry. These other methods offer higher sensitivity, specificity, and efficiency for protein sequencing. Sanger sequencing's main strength lies in its ability to accurately determine the sequence of DNA fragments, making it indispensable for DNA sequencing applications.

16.2 Determination of Secondary, Tertiary, and Quaternary Structures of Enzyme

Determining the secondary, tertiary, and quaternary structures of enzymes, as well as other proteins, is crucial for understanding their function and mechanism of action. Various experimental techniques are employed for this purpose, each offering unique insights into protein structure:

16.2.1 X-ray Crystallography:

X-ray crystallography is a powerful and widely used technique for determining the three-dimensional structure of enzymes at atomic resolution. It provides crucial insights into the spatial arrangement of atoms within an enzyme, revealing the intricate details of its active sites, substrate binding regions, and overall conformation. The process begins with the crystallization of the enzyme, a critical and often challenging step, as it requires the enzyme to form a highly ordered and stable crystal lattice. Crystals are formed by subjecting the enzyme solution to controlled conditions such as pH, temperature, and precipitant concentrations, which promote the slow aggregation of enzyme molecules into a solid crystalline form.

Once a crystal is obtained, it is subjected to X-rays in a process known as X-ray diffraction. The X-rays interact with the electrons of the atoms within the enzyme crystal, causing them to scatter or diffract. This diffraction pattern, consisting of numerous spots of varying intensities, is recorded by detectors surrounding the crystal. Each spot on the diffraction image corresponds to a specific plane within the crystal, providing information about the electron density distribution within the enzyme. By analysing the intensity and position of the diffraction spots, a detailed map of the electron density within the crystal can be constructed. This electron density map serves as a blueprint for building a three-dimensional atomic model of the enzyme. Using computational methods and known chemical properties of the enzyme, researchers fit the amino acid residues into the electron density to reconstruct the full structure. X-ray crystallography provides high-resolution data, often down to the angstrom level, enabling precise identification of the positions of individual atoms within the enzyme, including those involved in catalytic activity and substrate binding.

X-ray crystallography has been instrumental in advancing our understanding of enzyme mechanisms. By visualizing enzyme structures in their active or inactive states, it is possible to pinpoint the exact arrangement of catalytic residues and understand how enzymes facilitate chemical reactions. This technique has also been invaluable in drug design, where knowledge of the three-dimensional structure of target enzymes allows for the development of inhibitors or activators that fit precisely into the enzyme's active site.

Despite its powerful resolution, X-ray crystallography has limitations. Crystallization can be a difficult and time-consuming process, as not all enzymes readily form crystals, and some lose their functional conformation during crystallization. Additionally, the crystal structure represents a static snapshot of the enzyme, which may not fully capture the dynamic nature of enzyme activity in solution.

Nevertheless, X-ray crystallography remains the method of choice for determining the structure of enzymes, providing a window into their molecular architecture and enabling breakthroughs in enzyme engineering, drug discovery, and biochemistry. By elucidating the structural details of enzymes, X-ray crystallography continues to deepen our understanding of biological catalysis and expand the possibilities for designing enzymes with tailored functions.

16.2.2 Nuclear Magnetic Resonance (NMR) Spectroscopy:

Nuclear Magnetic Resonance (NMR) spectroscopy is a sophisticated and powerful technique used to determine the three-dimensional structure of enzymes and proteins in solution. Unlike X-ray crystallography, which provides static, high-resolution images of proteins in crystalline form, NMR spectroscopy offers a dynamic perspective by studying enzymes in their natural, solution-based environments. This makes NMR particularly valuable for analysing the flexibility, conformational changes, and molecular interactions of enzymes as they undergo their biological functions.

The principle behind NMR spectroscopy lies in the magnetic properties of atomic nuclei, particularly those with non-zero spin, such as hydrogen (^1H), carbon (^{13}C), and nitrogen (^{15}N). When placed in a strong magnetic field, these nuclei align with or against the field, existing in either a lower-energy or higher-energy state. By applying a pulse of radiofrequency (RF) energy, nuclei are excited to a higher-energy state, and as they relax back to their original state, they emit signals. These signals are detected and analysed to provide information about the chemical environment surrounding the nuclei, including distances and angles between them.

For protein structure determination, NMR spectroscopy typically focuses on atoms within the enzyme, primarily hydrogen (^1H), as these are abundant and highly sensitive to NMR. A series of NMR experiments, often multidimensional, are conducted to capture interactions between neighbouring atoms, including nuclear Overhauser effects (NOEs), which provide distance constraints between pairs of atoms. This data is then used to construct a three-dimensional model of the enzyme.

One of the key advantages of NMR spectroscopy is its ability to study proteins in their native, aqueous environments. This is crucial for understanding how enzymes behave under physiological conditions, providing insights into their flexibility, dynamics, and conformational changes. NMR can capture multiple states of an enzyme, such as different conformations during substrate binding, catalysis, or product release. This level of detail is particularly important for enzymes that undergo significant structural changes during their catalytic cycles.

NMR spectroscopy is also useful for studying enzyme-ligand interactions, including drug binding and allosteric regulation. By monitoring changes in NMR signals, researchers can map the binding sites of substrates, inhibitors, or activators, providing valuable information for drug design and enzyme engineering. Additionally, NMR can reveal how enzymes interact with other proteins or nucleic acids, offering insights into larger macromolecular complexes and their functions.

Despite its strengths, NMR spectroscopy has limitations. It is generally best suited for small to medium-sized proteins, typically up to around 40 kDa in molecular weight, as larger proteins produce complex, overlapping signals that are challenging to interpret. However, recent advancements in isotope labelling (e.g., ^{13}C and ^{15}N labelling) and cryogenic probe technology have expanded the range of proteins that can be studied using NMR.

Another limitation is the time-consuming nature of NMR experiments, which can take days or weeks to collect sufficient data for structure determination. Additionally, while NMR provides lower resolution compared to X-ray crystallography, it excels in offering a dynamic view of proteins in solution, capturing the motions and conformational changes that are essential for enzyme function.

NMR spectroscopy has been instrumental in advancing the understanding of enzymes, particularly in fields such as enzyme dynamics, drug discovery, and protein-protein interactions. It complements other structural biology techniques, such as X-ray crystallography and cryo-electron microscopy (cryo-EM), providing a fuller picture of enzyme structure and function. By enabling the study of enzymes in their native environments, NMR offers unique insights into the molecular mechanisms that drive biological catalysis and regulation.

16.2.3 Cryo-Electron Microscopy (Cryo-EM):

Cryo-electron microscopy (Cryo-EM) has revolutionized the field of structural biology, offering a powerful method for visualizing the structures of large and complex biomolecules, including enzymes, without the need for crystallization. This cutting-edge technique involves flash-freezing protein samples in a thin layer of vitreous ice, preserving their native states, and imaging them using an electron microscope. Cryo-EM has become particularly valuable for studying large protein complexes, flexible structures, and heterogeneous samples that are difficult or impossible to crystallize.

The process begins with the rapid freezing of a protein solution at cryogenic temperatures, typically around -180°C, which prevents the formation of ice crystals that could damage the sample or interfere with imaging. Instead, the water forms vitreous ice, a glass-like, non-crystalline state that preserves the native conformation of the enzyme molecules. The sample is then placed under the electron microscope, where a beam of electrons is passed through it, generating detailed images of the enzyme from different angles.

One of the key strengths of Cryo-EM is its ability to capture high-resolution, three-dimensional structures of enzymes in their near-native environments. Unlike X-ray crystallography, which requires the formation of crystals and often provides only a static snapshot of the enzyme, Cryo-EM can visualize enzymes in multiple conformational states. This is especially useful for studying dynamic and flexible enzymes that undergo structural changes during their catalytic cycles, as Cryo-EM can capture different functional states, providing a more comprehensive understanding of enzyme mechanisms.

Cryo-EM has also overcome many of the size limitations that affect techniques like NMR spectroscopy. It is particularly well-suited for studying large enzymes and macromolecular complexes, such as multi-enzyme assemblies, membrane-bound enzymes, and even viral particles. This capability has made it an indispensable tool for researchers investigating the structure of challenging targets, such as membrane proteins and large multi-subunit enzymes.

In addition to its ability to handle large and flexible samples, Cryo-EM does not require the crystallization of the enzyme, which is often a time-consuming and difficult process. Many enzymes, especially those that are highly flexible or exist in multiple conformational states, are notoriously difficult to crystallize. Cryo-EM bypasses this requirement, allowing for the direct observation of these enzymes in their native states.

Recent advancements in Cryo-EM technology, including the development of direct electron detectors and improved image processing algorithms, have significantly increased the resolution of Cryo-EM structures. With these improvements, Cryo-EM can now produce near-atomic resolution images, rivalling X-ray crystallography in many cases. This has led to a surge in the number of high-resolution enzyme structures solved using Cryo-EM, making it a go-to technique for structural biologists.

Cryo-EM has had a profound impact on a wide range of scientific fields, from enzymology to drug discovery. By providing detailed insights into the structure and function of enzymes, Cryo-EM has facilitated the design of new drugs that target specific enzymes involved in diseases. It has also advanced our understanding of enzyme mechanisms, helping researchers explore how enzymes catalyse reactions, interact with substrates, and respond to regulatory molecules.

Despite its many advantages, Cryo-EM also has some limitations. One challenge is the relatively low contrast of biological samples, as proteins consist primarily of light atoms (carbon, nitrogen, oxygen), which scatter electrons weakly compared to heavier elements. This makes it difficult to visualize small proteins with Cryo-EM, although advances in sample preparation and image processing are continually improving the technique's sensitivity. Additionally, while Cryo-EM excels at studying large proteins, it can be less effective for very small enzymes or those with limited structural features.

Overall, Cryo-EM has transformed the field of structural biology by making it possible to determine the structures of large, complex, and dynamic enzyme systems with unprecedented detail. Its ability to capture enzymes in multiple states and without the need for crystallization has opened up new frontiers in understanding enzyme structure, function, and regulation, offering promising applications in biotechnology, medicine, and beyond.

Each of these techniques has its strengths and limitations, and researchers often employ a combination of methods to obtain a comprehensive understanding of protein structure and function. By elucidating the secondary, tertiary, and quaternary structures of enzymes, scientists can gain valuable insights into how these proteins catalyse biochemical reactions and interact with other molecules in the cell.

CHAPTER XVII

Ribozymes

Ribozymes, short for "ribonucleic acid enzymes," are RNA molecules that possess the remarkable ability to catalyse chemical reactions, much like protein-based enzymes. This discovery revolutionized our understanding of molecular biology, revealing that RNA is not merely a passive carrier of genetic information but also an active participant in cellular processes. First discovered in the early 1980s by Thomas Cech and Sidney Altman, ribozymes challenged the dogma that only proteins could catalyse biochemical reactions, earning the scientists the Nobel Prize in Chemistry in 1989. Since then, ribozymes have become central to the study of molecular evolution, RNA biology, and potential therapeutic applications.

17.1 Structure and Mechanism of Ribozymes

Ribozymes, like proteins, fold into specific three-dimensional structures that are essential for their catalytic activity. The structure of ribozymes can vary widely depending on the type and function, but generally, they contain regions of base pairing and unpaired nucleotides that help form the active site. Some ribozymes possess highly intricate secondary and tertiary structures, with loops, bulges, and pseudoknots creating the catalytic core.

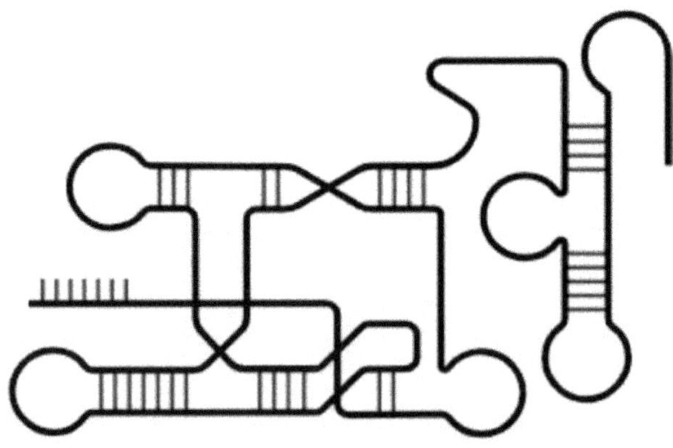

Figure 1 Structure of Ribozyme

The catalytic mechanism of ribozymes, while similar in principle to protein enzymes, involves the RNA's ability to fold and create binding pockets for substrates. The ribozyme's catalytic activity is often facilitated by the formation of hydrogen bonds, electrostatic interactions, and the use of metal ions, particularly magnesium (Mg^{2+}), to stabilize the transition state or activate water molecules for hydrolysis reactions.

The most well-known catalytic mechanisms employed by ribozymes include:

- **Phosphodiester Bond Cleavage**: Many ribozymes catalyse the cleavage of RNA phosphodiester bonds through a transesterification reaction. For instance, the hammerhead and hairpin ribozymes catalyse self-cleavage reactions.
- **Peptidyl Transferase Activity**: In the ribosome, the RNA component catalyses peptide bond formation during protein synthesis. This function is performed by the ribosomal RNA (rRNA) in the ribosome, which is considered a large ribozyme.

17.2 Types of Ribozymes

Several classes of ribozymes have been identified, each with specific catalytic functions. These ribozymes vary in size, structure, and biological role:

17.2.1 Small Self-Cleaving Ribozymes

These ribozymes catalyse reactions within their own sequence. The best-known examples include:

17.2.1.1 Hammerhead Ribozyme

The hammerhead ribozyme was initially discovered in plant viroids, which are small, circular RNA pathogens. This ribozyme catalyses self-cleavage of RNA through a unique structure composed of three stems (helix I, II, and III) that form a conserved catalytic core. The cleavage occurs at a specific phosphodiester bond in the RNA backbone, facilitating a transesterification reaction that breaks the RNA strand. The hammerhead ribozyme's ability to perform precise self-cleavage has made it a valuable tool for studying RNA catalysis and has potential applications in gene therapy and molecular biology.

17.2.1.2 Hairpin Ribozyme

The hairpin ribozyme was first identified in the satellite RNA of plant viruses, where it catalyses a site-specific RNA cleavage and ligation reaction.

Its structure includes two interacting loops that form a catalytic core responsible for facilitating the cleavage reaction. Unlike many other ribozymes, the hairpin ribozyme does not require metal ions for its catalytic activity, relying instead on precise RNA folding and interactions. This ribozyme serves as a model system for RNA folding studies and is used in various molecular biology applications.

17.2.1.3 HDV Ribozyme (Hepatitis Delta Virus)

The HDV ribozyme, found in the hepatitis delta virus, plays a critical role in the virus's replication cycle by catalysing the self-cleavage of its RNA genome. The HDV ribozyme exhibits a highly compact and stable structure, which facilitates the cleavage of phosphodiester bonds within the viral RNA. The HDV ribozyme's catalytic efficiency and its involvement in a human pathogen have made it a target for antiviral therapeutic strategies and a subject of extensive structural and mechanistic research.

17.3 Group I and Group II Introns

These are larger ribozymes found in the introns of genes. They catalyse their own splicing from precursor RNA molecules during RNA processing.

17.3.1 Group I Introns

Group I introns are catalytic RNA molecules that facilitate self-splicing reactions without the need for protein enzymes. They do so by initiating a nucleophilic attack by an external guanosine cofactor on the RNA's phosphodiester backbone. This reaction cleaves the RNA at specific sites, excising the intron and ligating the exons. Group I introns are found in the nuclear, mitochondrial, and chloroplast genomes of various organisms, including fungi, protists, and plants. Due to their self-splicing activity, Group I introns serve as models for studying RNA catalysis and evolution. They also have potential applications in biotechnology, particularly for RNA manipulation and gene editing.

17.3.2 Group II Introns

Group II introns are self-splicing RNA elements that catalyse their excision through a mechanism remarkably similar to the spliceosome-mediated splicing of eukaryotic pre-mRNAs. The splicing involves the formation of a lariat intermediate, where a specific nucleotide within the intron attacks the phosphodiester bond at the intron-exon junction, leading to cleavage and ligation of the exons. Group II introns are found in the mitochondrial and chloroplast genomes of plants, fungi, and some bacteria. These introns are thought to be evolutionary precursors to the spliceosome, the complex responsible for RNA splicing in higher organisms. Their ability to self-splice has led to their exploration as tools for gene targeting, as well as their use in evolutionary studies to understand the origins of complex RNA-processing systems.

17.4. Ribosomal RNA (rRNA)

One of the most essential ribozymes in cellular biology is the large subunit rRNA in the ribosome. The ribosome is composed of both RNA and proteins, but it is the RNA portion that catalyses the formation of peptide bonds during protein synthesis. The **peptidyl transferase centre** of the ribosome is an RNA-based catalyst, making the ribosome a large, complex ribozyme.

17.5 Catalytic Mechanism

Ribozymes catalyse reactions through various mechanisms, many of which are strikingly similar to those used by protein enzymes. These mechanisms involve:

- **Acid-Base Catalysis**: Ribozymes often use specific nucleotide bases within their structure to act as acid or base catalysts. In many cases, the 2' hydroxyl group of ribose participates in nucleophilic attack.
- **Metal Ion Catalysis**: Ribozymes frequently utilize metal ions (often Mg^{2+}) to stabilize negative charges that develop during catalysis, assist in substrate binding, and facilitate catalytic activity. Metal ions can act as cofactors and stabilize the transition state of reactions.
- **Conformational Changes**: Many ribozymes undergo significant conformational changes upon binding their substrates, which helps position the reactive groups for catalysis and lowers the activation energy of the reaction.

17.6 Role of Ribozymes in Evolution and Origin of Life

Ribozymes have provided crucial insights into the **RNA World Hypothesis**, which postulates that early life forms may have relied solely on RNA for both genetic information storage and catalytic activity. This hypothesis suggests that before the evolution of proteins, ribozymes could have catalysed key biochemical reactions necessary for life, such as self-replication and metabolism.

The discovery that RNA molecules can act as catalysts supports the idea that RNA played a central role in the origin of life. The ability of ribozymes to evolve and acquire new functions also mimics Darwinian evolution, with RNA capable of undergoing mutations, selection, and amplification to produce molecules with enhanced catalytic functions.

17.7. Applications of Ribozymes

The catalytic properties of ribozymes have opened up several potential biotechnological and therapeutic applications:

17.7.1. Therapeutic Applications

Ribozymes have shown promise as therapeutic agents, especially for their ability to target and cleave specific RNA sequences. This has potential in treating viral infections, genetic disorders, and cancer:

- **Antiviral Therapy**: Ribozymes can be designed to cleave viral RNA genomes, potentially blocking viral replication. For example, ribozymes have been explored as treatments for HIV, hepatitis, and other viral diseases.
- **Gene Therapy**: In gene therapy, ribozymes can be engineered to target and degrade mRNAs produced from mutated genes, thereby reducing the expression of harmful proteins.

17.7.2. Biotechnological Applications

Ribozymes have found utility in biotechnology as molecular tools for RNA manipulation and gene expression control:

- **RNA Processing Tools**: Ribozymes can be used to catalyse the cleavage and ligation of RNA molecules in vitro, making them useful in synthetic biology and genetic engineering.
- **Biosensors**: Ribozymes have been incorporated into biosensors to detect specific RNA sequences or other small molecules, providing a platform for diagnostic applications.

Ribozymes represent a fascinating class of catalytic RNA molecules that blur the lines between genetic information carriers and enzymes. From their central role in the ribosome to their applications in gene therapy, ribozymes have had a profound impact on our understanding of molecular biology and biotechnology. Ongoing research into ribozyme structure, function, and applications promises to further unlock their potential, offering novel solutions to both fundamental biological questions and pressing medical challenges. The discovery of ribozymes remains one of the most significant findings in the field of biochemistry, with implications that continue to unfold across diverse scientific disciplines.

CHAPTER XVIII

Abzymes (Catalytic Antibodies)

Abzymes, also known as catalytic antibodies, are engineered antibodies that function as enzymes, catalyzing specific chemical reactions. The term "abzyme" is a portmanteau of "antibody" and "enzyme." Abzymes represent a unique intersection of immunology and enzymology, harnessing the specificity of antibodies with the catalytic properties of enzymes. These molecules are created by exploiting the natural binding properties of antibodies and designing them to act on transition-state analogues of chemical reactions. Since their discovery, abzymes have opened new avenues for biocatalysis, drug development, and therapeutic interventions. This chapter delves into the mechanisms, generation, applications, and future potential of abzymes, highlighting their significance in both research and clinical settings.

18.1 Discovery of Abzymes

The concept of catalytic antibodies was first proposed by Nobel laureate Linus Pauling in the 1940s, who theorized that antibodies could potentially stabilize transition states of chemical reactions. However, it wasn't until the 1980s that the first abzyme was experimentally generated. Peter Schultz and colleagues successfully created antibodies that could catalyse a chemical reaction by using a transition-state analogue to immunize animals, thus producing antibodies capable of lowering the activation energy of the reaction. This was a revolutionary achievement that established the proof of concept for abzymes and set the stage for further research into catalytic antibodies.

18.2 Mechanism of Abzyme Action

Abzymes operate based on the same fundamental principles as natural enzymes: they accelerate chemical reactions by stabilizing the transition state, thereby lowering the activation energy. However, abzymes differ from natural enzymes in that they are derived from the immune system rather than cellular processes. The mechanism of abzyme catalysis involves several key steps:

18.2.1 Binding to the Transition-State Analog: The immune system generates antibodies that recognize and bind to specific antigens. In the case of abzymes, the antigen used to stimulate antibody production is a transition-state analogue, a stable molecule that mimics the structure of the reaction's transition state. These antibodies are selected for their ability to bind strongly to this analogue.

18.2.2 Stabilization of the Transition State: Once an abzyme binds to the substrate, it stabilizes the transition state of the reaction, reducing the activation energy needed for the reaction to proceed. This stabilization is key to the abzyme's catalytic activity, as it allows the reaction to occur more efficiently.

18.2.3 Catalysis of the Reaction: After stabilizing the transition state, the abzyme facilitates the conversion of the substrate into the product, much like a natural enzyme. The abzyme can then release the product and bind to another substrate molecule, continuing the catalytic cycle.

18.3. Generation of Abzymes

The process of generating abzymes involves several steps, typically starting with the selection of a chemical reaction of interest and identifying a transition-state analogue. Below is a detailed breakdown of how abzymes are generated:

18.3.1 Transition-State Analog Design

The design of an effective transition-state analogue is critical to the creation of a successful abzyme. A transition-state analogue is a stable compound that resembles the high-energy, unstable intermediate formed during a chemical reaction. Because transition states are short-lived and difficult to isolate, analogues are used to mimic the structure of the transition state.

- **Structure Mimicry:** The transition-state analogue must closely resemble the geometry and electronic properties of the transition state. This mimicry ensures that the immune system generates antibodies with high affinity for the transition state, leading to the production of catalytically active abzymes.

- **Chemical Stability:** Since transition states are fleeting, the analogue must be chemically stable enough to withstand the immunization process and stimulate antibody production without undergoing degradation.

18.3.2 Immunization and Antibody Production

Once a suitable transition-state analogue is designed, the next step is to immunize an animal (such as a mouse or rabbit) with the analogue.

The immune system responds by producing antibodies that recognize the transition-state analogue as a foreign molecule (antigen). These antibodies are harvested from the animal's serum and screened for catalytic activity.

- **Polyclonal and Monoclonal Antibodies:** Initially, polyclonal antibodies (a mixture of antibodies) are produced. However, to obtain highly specific abzymes, monoclonal antibodies are preferred. Monoclonal antibodies are generated from a single B cell clone, ensuring uniformity in the antibodies' structure and catalytic function.
- **Hybridoma Technology:** To generate monoclonal antibodies, the hybridoma technique is commonly used. This technique involves fusing antibody-producing B cells with immortalized myeloma cells to create hybrid cells that continuously produce the desired antibody.

18.3.3 Screening for Catalytic Activity

After antibody production, the next step is to screen for catalytic activity. Not all antibodies produced will have the desired catalytic properties, so high-throughput screening methods are employed to identify antibodies that can catalyse the reaction of interest. These assays measure the rate of reaction in the presence of the antibody and compare it to a control reaction without the antibody.

- **Kinetic Parameters:** Once a catalytically active abzyme is identified, its kinetic parameters, such as the Michaelis constant (K_m) and maximum velocity (V_{max}), are determined. These parameters provide insights into the efficiency and affinity of the abzyme for its substrate.

18.4. Types of Abzymes

Abzymes can catalyse a wide range of chemical reactions, from simple bond cleavage to more complex transformations. The versatility of abzymes has been demonstrated in various reaction types, including:

18.4.1 Hydrolytic Abzymes

Hydrolytic abzymes catalyse the cleavage of chemical bonds through the addition of water, similar to natural hydrolases. These abzymes have been developed to catalyse reactions such as ester hydrolysis, peptide bond cleavage, and phosphate ester hydrolysis.

- **Esterase Activity:** Some abzymes have been designed to catalyse the hydrolysis of ester bonds, making them useful in organic synthesis and pharmaceutical development.
- **Protease Activity:** Abzymes with protease-like activity have been engineered to cleave peptide bonds, offering potential applications in protein engineering and therapeutic protein degradation.

18.4.2 Redox Abzymes

Redox abzymes catalyse oxidation-reduction (redox) reactions, where electrons are transferred between molecules. These reactions are crucial in cellular metabolism and energy production.

- **Oxidative Reactions:** Abzymes capable of catalysing oxidative reactions have potential applications in biosensing and environmental detoxification.

18.4.3 Diels-Alder Abzymes

Diels-Alder reactions, a type of cycloaddition reaction, are widely used in synthetic organic chemistry to form carbon-carbon bonds. Abzymes have been developed to catalyse Diels-Alder reactions, allowing for the creation of complex molecular structures with high specificity and efficiency.

- **Stereoselectivity:** Abzymes can be designed to catalyse Diels-Alder reactions with high stereoselectivity, making them valuable tools in the synthesis of enantiomerically pure compounds.

18.4.4 Carbon-Carbon Bond Formation

Carbon-carbon bond formation is a critical step in many chemical syntheses. Abzymes capable of catalysing these reactions have been developed for use in organic chemistry and drug development.

18.5. Applications of Abzymes

The ability of abzymes to catalyse specific reactions has led to their exploration in various fields, including biotechnology, medicine, and industry. Below are some of the key applications of abzymes:

18.5.1 Therapeutic Applications

One of the most promising applications of abzymes is in the development of novel therapeutic agents. Because abzymes can be engineered to catalyse specific reactions, they have the potential to target disease-causing molecules with high precision.

- **HIV Therapy:** Abzymes have been developed that target and cleave the viral proteins of HIV, offering potential as antiviral agents. By specifically targeting viral proteins, abzymes could provide a new strategy for combating viral infections.
- **Cancer Therapy:** Abzymes have been explored for their ability to selectively target and degrade oncogenic proteins, providing a potential approach for cancer treatment.

18.5.2 Industrial and Environmental Applications

Abzymes have potential applications in industrial catalysis and environmental remediation. Their specificity and catalytic efficiency make them attractive candidates for use in biocatalysis, where they can replace traditional chemical catalysts.

- **Green Chemistry:** Abzymes can be used to catalyse chemical reactions under mild conditions, reducing the need for harsh chemicals and high temperatures. This makes them suitable for environmentally friendly chemical processes.
- **Pollutant Degradation:** Abzymes that catalyse the breakdown of environmental pollutants, such as pesticides and industrial waste, offer potential solutions for environmental cleanup.

18.5.3 Diagnostic Tools

The specificity of abzymes can be harnessed in diagnostic assays. Abzymes that catalyse reactions in the presence of specific biomolecules can be used to detect disease markers, pathogens, or environmental contaminants.

- **Biosensors:** Abzyme-based biosensors have been developed for the detection of small molecules, proteins, and nucleic acids. These biosensors are highly sensitive and can be used in clinical diagnostics or environmental monitoring.

18.6. Limitations of Abzymes

Despite their potential, abzymes face several challenges that have limited their widespread use.

18.6.1 Catalytic Efficiency

Abzymes generally exhibit lower catalytic efficiency compared to natural enzymes. This is partly due to the limited chemical diversity of the amino acid residues in the antibody active site, which may not be as optimized for catalysis as the active sites of natural enzymes.

18.6.2 Stability

Abzymes may lack the stability of natural enzymes, particularly under extreme conditions such as high temperatures or varying pH levels. This can limit their practical applications in industrial processes where robust catalysts are required.

18.6.3 Immunogenicity

As abzymes are derived from antibodies, they may elicit an immune response when used in therapeutic applications. The immunogenicity of abzymes needs to be carefully considered and minimized to avoid adverse reactions in patients.

Abzymes, or catalytic antibodies, are a unique class of biocatalysts that combine the specificity of antibodies with the catalytic power of enzymes. They offer exciting opportunities in diverse fields, from drug development and therapeutics to industrial catalysis and environmental applications. While challenges remain, ongoing research and advancements in antibody engineering, transition-state analogue design, and catalysis are likely to further expand the utility of abzymes in the coming years. By harnessing the catalytic potential of antibodies, abzymes could revolutionize both biotechnology and medicine, offering new strategies for disease treatment, green chemistry, and beyond.

CHAPTER XIX

Purification of Enzymes

Enzyme purification is a critical process in biochemistry, essential for studying the structure, function, and applications of enzymes in both research and industry. Enzymes, being proteins, often exist in complex biological mixtures alongside other proteins, nucleic acids, lipids, and small molecules. Therefore, to isolate and analyse a specific enzyme, a purification process must be employed. The goal of enzyme purification is to obtain an enzyme preparation with the highest possible activity and purity while maintaining its structural integrity and functional properties. The purified enzyme can then be studied for its kinetic properties, three-dimensional structure, regulatory mechanisms, and potential biotechnological applications. This chapter covers the fundamental principles, methods, and steps involved in enzyme purification, focusing on both classical and modern techniques. Various strategies and methods used to isolate and purify enzymes from natural sources or recombinant expression systems will be explained in detail.

19.1 Principles of Enzyme Purification

The basic principle of enzyme purification involves exploiting the unique physical and chemical properties of the target enzyme, such as its size, charge, solubility, hydrophobicity, and affinity for specific ligands. Enzyme purification is typically performed in several steps, gradually increasing the purity and concentration of the enzyme. Common techniques employed during purification include centrifugation, precipitation, chromatography, electrophoresis, and ultrafiltration. Each step of the purification process is designed to separate the enzyme from contaminants while minimizing the loss of enzyme activity.

The efficiency of the purification process is typically measured by three key parameters:

- **Specific Activity**: The enzyme activity per unit of protein, often expressed in terms of micromoles of substrate converted per minute per milligram of protein.
- **Yield**: The percentage of enzyme activity recovered after each purification step.

- **Purification Fold**: The ratio of specific activity after purification to the specific activity of the crude extract.

19.1.1 Factors Influencing Enzyme Purification
Several factors can affect the success of enzyme purification, including:

- **Source of the enzyme**: Enzymes may be derived from tissues, microbial cultures, or recombinant expression systems, and the purification strategy can vary depending on the source.
- **Enzyme stability**: Many enzymes are sensitive to factors such as temperature, pH, and the presence of proteases, which can lead to denaturation or degradation during purification. Therefore, purification protocols often involve buffers and stabilizers to preserve enzyme activity.
- **Concentration of enzyme**: Some enzymes may be present in low abundance in the source material, requiring concentration techniques in the early steps of purification.
- **Detection and assay**: Enzyme activity assays or other detection methods must be available to monitor the presence and purity of the enzyme during purification.

19.2 Steps Involved in Enzyme Purification
The purification of enzymes typically involves multiple steps, each progressively increasing the purity of the enzyme. These steps are optimized based on the enzyme's properties and the type of contaminants present.

19.2.1. Source Selection and Cell Disruption
The first step in enzyme purification is selecting the biological source of the enzyme, which can be animal tissues, plant materials, microbial cultures, or recombinant systems. Once the source is identified, the cells or tissues are disrupted to release the enzyme into solution. Several methods can be used to achieve this:

19.2.1.1 Mechanical Disruption
Mechanical disruption is a physical method used to break open cells and release intracellular contents, including enzymes. Techniques such as **homogenization, sonication,** and **French press** are commonly employed.

- **Homogenization** involves grinding or shearing cells in a buffer, which ruptures the cell membrane.
- **Sonication** uses high-frequency sound waves to create cavitation, causing the cells to burst.
- The **French press** forces cells through a narrow valve under high pressure, leading to mechanical lysis.

These methods are effective for disrupting a wide range of cells, from microbial to animal tissues, and are often used in the initial stages of enzyme purification.

19.2.1.2 Enzymatic Digestion

Enzymatic digestion uses specific enzymes to break down cell walls and release intracellular components. For example, **lysozyme** is used to degrade bacterial cell walls by cleaving peptidoglycan, while **cellulase** breaks down the cellulose in plant cell walls. This method is typically mild, minimizing damage to sensitive proteins and enzymes. Enzymatic digestion is particularly useful for organisms with robust cell walls, like bacteria and plants, as it avoids the harsh conditions of mechanical disruption.

19.2.1.3 Chemical Lysis

Chemical lysis involves the use of detergents, chaotropic agents, or other chemicals to solubilize cell membranes and release intracellular enzymes. Detergents like **Triton X-100** or **SDS** disrupt lipid bilayers, while **chaotropic agents** (e.g., urea, guanidine hydrochloride) denature proteins and solubilize membranes. This method is often used when mechanical or enzymatic techniques are insufficient, especially for difficult-to-lyse cells. However, chemical lysis must be carefully controlled to avoid denaturing the enzyme of interest.

The crude extract obtained from cell disruption contains a mixture of proteins, including the target enzyme, as well as nucleic acids, lipids, and other cellular components. This extract is the starting material for further purification steps.

19.2.2 Clarification by Centrifugation and Filtration

Once the cells are disrupted, the crude extract is clarified to remove insoluble debris, organelles, and unbroken cells. This is typically done by **centrifugation** at low speed, which pelts the insoluble material while leaving the enzyme in the supernatant. The clarified extract is then passed through filtration systems, such as membrane filters, to remove fine particulate matter and further clarify the enzyme solution.

19.2.3. Enzyme Precipitation

Precipitation is one of the oldest and simplest methods for enzyme purification. The principle behind precipitation is that proteins can be selectively precipitated out of solution by altering the solubility of proteins through changes in factors such as pH, ionic strength, or temperature. Some common precipitation methods include:

19.2.3.1 Ammonium Sulphate Precipitation

Ammonium sulphate precipitation is a widely used technique to purify enzymes based on their solubility in high salt concentrations. Ammonium sulphate is added gradually to the enzyme solution, causing proteins to "salt out" or precipitate due to the reduced solubility. Proteins and enzymes exhibit different solubility characteristics, so fractional precipitation can isolate specific enzymes by adjusting the concentration of ammonium sulphate. This method is particularly useful in the early stages of purification, as it allows for the concentration of the enzyme and the removal of unwanted proteins from the mixture.

19.2.3.2 Organic Solvent Precipitation

Organic solvent precipitation involves the use of solvents such as ethanol or acetone to precipitate enzymes. The addition of these solvents reduces the water activity in the solution, causing proteins to aggregate and precipitate out. This method is generally carried out at low temperatures to maintain enzyme stability, as organic solvents can denature proteins if not properly controlled. Organic solvent precipitation is commonly used in conjunction with other purification methods to isolate enzymes based on their solubility profiles.

19.2.3.3 Isoelectric Precipitation

In **isoelectric precipitation**, the pH of the enzyme solution is adjusted to the enzyme's **isoelectric point (pI)**, the pH at which the enzyme has no net electrical charge. At this point, the enzyme is least soluble and tends to precipitate out of solution. This method takes advantage of the fact that proteins have different isoelectric points, allowing for selective precipitation of the enzyme of interest. Isoelectric precipitation is often used to purify enzymes with distinct pI values from other proteins in the solution.

Precipitation is generally followed by dialysis or ultrafiltration to remove excess salts or solvents and to concentrate the enzyme solution.

19.2.4. Chromatography Techniques

Chromatography is the most versatile and widely used method for enzyme purification. There are several types of chromatography based on different physical and chemical properties of enzymes:

19.2.4.1. Ion Exchange Chromatography

Ion exchange chromatography is a powerful technique used to separate proteins based on their net charge at a specific pH. This method involves passing a protein solution through a column containing a resin with charged groups. Proteins with charges opposite to the resin's groups bind to the resin (anion or cation exchangers), while those with similar charges are not retained. The bound proteins are then eluted by gradually increasing the salt concentration or altering the pH, which competes with the proteins for binding sites on the resin. This technique is highly effective for separating proteins with different charge properties and is widely used in both research and industrial applications for enzyme purification.

19.2.4.2. Gel Filtration (Size Exclusion) Chromatography

Gel filtration chromatography, also known as size exclusion chromatography, separates proteins based on their size. In this technique, the enzyme solution is passed through a column packed with porous beads. Small molecules and proteins enter the pores of the beads and thus travel more slowly through the column, while larger proteins are excluded from the pores and elute faster. This results in separation based on size, with larger proteins emerging from the column before smaller ones. Gel filtration is particularly useful for the final polishing of enzyme preparations and for determining the molecular weight of the enzyme. It provides a gentle separation method that helps maintain protein activity and stability.

19.2.4.3 Affinity Chromatography

Affinity chromatography is a highly specific technique that separates proteins based on their interaction with a particular ligand, substrate, or inhibitor immobilized on a resin. The target enzyme binds to the ligand with high specificity, while other proteins are washed away. Elution of the bound enzyme is achieved by adding a free form of the ligand or by altering buffer conditions to disrupt the enzyme-ligand interaction. This method offers high specificity and purity and is particularly useful for purifying recombinant enzymes with affinity tags such as His-tag or GST-tag. Affinity chromatography is often used to achieve high levels of enzyme purity and is a critical tool in both research and industrial enzyme production.

19.2.4.4 Hydrophobic Interaction Chromatography (HIC)

Hydrophobic interaction chromatography (HIC) separates proteins based on their hydrophobicity. In this method, proteins are applied to a column containing a hydrophobic resin at high salt concentrations. The high salt environment enhances the hydrophobic interactions between the proteins and the resin, leading to the binding of proteins with exposed hydrophobic regions. Elution is achieved by gradually decreasing the salt concentration, which reduces hydrophobic interactions and allows proteins to detach from the resin. HIC is useful for the separation of proteins with different hydrophobic properties and is often employed as a polishing step in protein purification processes to achieve higher purity and concentration.

19.2.5 Ultrafiltration and Concentration

After chromatographic separation, enzyme solutions may be diluted, requiring concentration for further analysis or application. **Ultrafiltration** is a widely utilized method for this purpose, employing membranes with specific pore sizes to selectively retain large molecules, such as proteins, while allowing smaller molecules and solvents to pass through. This process effectively concentrates the enzyme solution by removing excess solvent and small contaminants, thus increasing the enzyme's concentration.

Ultrafiltration is not only valuable for concentrating enzyme preparations but also for buffer exchange. By employing membranes with appropriate molecular weight cutoffs, the technique facilitates the removal of salts, small molecules, and other impurities while simultaneously replacing the buffer system with a desired one. This dual functionality makes ultrafiltration an essential step in the purification process, ensuring that the enzyme is prepared in a suitable buffer and at the desired concentration for subsequent studies or applications.

19.2.6. Electrophoresis

Electrophoresis is a crucial analytical technique used to assess enzyme purity and monitor the progress of enzyme purification. Among the various electrophoresis methods, **polyacrylamide gel electrophoresis (PAGE)** is particularly valuable. In **SDS-PAGE (Sodium Dodecyl Sulfate-Polyacrylamide Gel Electrophoresis)**, proteins are separated based on their molecular weight. The process involves denaturing proteins with SDS, which imparts a uniform negative charge, allowing the proteins to migrate through a polyacrylamide gel in proportion to their size when subjected to an electric field. SDS-PAGE provides a clear estimate of the enzyme's molecular weight and can reveal the presence of contaminants or degradation products by showing discrete bands corresponding to different proteins.

In addition to SDS-PAGE, **Native PAGE** is employed to assess the enzyme's native conformation and functionality. Unlike SDS-PAGE, native PAGE maintains the enzyme's native structure and charge state, allowing the observation of enzyme activity in the gel. This method helps confirm that the enzyme retains its functional properties after purification, ensuring that it has not been denatured or otherwise altered during the process. Both SDS-PAGE and Native PAGE are instrumental in evaluating enzyme purity, structural integrity, and functional status, providing essential insights into the success of the purification process.

19.3. Characterization of Purified Enzymes

After purification, the enzyme is typically subjected to several assays to determine its activity, kinetic properties, and structural integrity. Common characterization methods include:

19.3.1 Enzyme Activity Assays

Enzyme activity assays are fundamental for assessing the functional capability of an enzyme to catalyse a specific biochemical reaction. These assays typically involve monitoring the conversion of substrates into products, often measured using spectrophotometry or fluorometry. Spectrophotometric assays measure changes in absorbance due to the formation or consumption of light-absorbing species, while fluorometric assays detect changes in fluorescence, providing high sensitivity. Activity assays are crucial for evaluating enzyme performance, optimizing purification processes, and determining enzyme kinetics.

19.3.2 Kinetic Studies

Kinetic studies provide essential information about an enzyme's catalytic efficiency and substrate affinity. By analysing the enzyme's Michaelis constant (K_m) and maximum velocity (V_{max}), these studies reveal how effectively an enzyme binds to its substrate and its maximum catalytic rate. K_m represents the substrate concentration at which the reaction rate is half of V_{max}, indicating the enzyme's affinity for the substrate. V_{max} is the maximum rate of reaction when the enzyme is fully saturated with substrate. Kinetic studies help in understanding enzyme mechanisms and optimizing conditions for industrial applications.

19.3.3 Molecular Weight Determination

Molecular weight determination is a key step in characterizing an enzyme's size and confirming its purity. Techniques such as **SDS-PAGE**

(sodium dodecyl sulphate-polyacrylamide gel electrophoresis) separate proteins based on their molecular weight, providing an estimate of the enzyme's size. **Gel filtration chromatography** separates proteins based on size, allowing for molecular weight estimation and further purification. **Mass spectrometry** offers precise molecular weight measurements and detailed information about the enzyme's structure and post-translational modifications. Accurate molecular weight determination is essential for enzyme identification and characterization.

19.3.4 Spectroscopic Analysis

Spectroscopic analysis provides insights into the enzyme's structure, folding, and stability. **UV-visible spectroscopy** monitors changes in absorbance related to chromophores within the enzyme, aiding in assessing enzyme concentration and interaction with substrates or inhibitors. **Fluorescence spectroscopy** offers information on enzyme dynamics and conformational changes by measuring fluorescence emitted from intrinsic or extrinsic probes. **Circular dichroism (CD) spectroscopy** evaluates the enzyme's secondary structure by analysing the differential absorption of left- and right-circularly polarized light, providing information on protein folding and stability. These techniques are vital for understanding enzyme structure-function relationships and stability under different conditions.

Enzyme purification is a vital process in both scientific research and industrial applications. The methods and techniques used to purify enzymes, from precipitation and centrifugation to advanced chromatography and ultrafiltration, are crucial for isolating enzymes with high purity and activity. As enzyme research progresses, the refinement and innovation of purification techniques will continue to play a central role in understanding enzyme function, developing novel biocatalysts, and applying enzymes to solve global challenges in health, industry, and the environment.

CHAPTER XX

Application of Enzymes in Agriculture

Enzymes have become an integral part of modern agriculture, providing innovative solutions to improve crop yield, soil fertility, pest control, and the sustainability of farming practices. Enzymes are biological catalysts that accelerate biochemical reactions in living organisms. In agriculture, they are utilized for their ability to enhance nutrient availability, improve plant growth, break down organic matter, and protect crops from diseases. The application of enzymes in agriculture not only supports more efficient farming practices but also aligns with the growing demand for environmentally friendly and sustainable approaches to food production.

20.1. Role of Enzymes in Soil Health and Fertility

Soil health is fundamental to successful agriculture, and enzymes play a crucial role in maintaining its fertility. Soil enzymes, produced by microorganisms, plants, and fungi, help in the decomposition of organic matter, thereby releasing essential nutrients such as nitrogen, phosphorus, and sulfur for plant uptake. These enzymes include phosphatases, ureases, and dehydrogenases, each contributing to the nutrient cycling processes in soil ecosystems.

- **Phosphatases** break down organic phosphorus compounds, making phosphorus available for plant uptake. Phosphorus is critical for energy transfer, photosynthesis, and other biochemical reactions in plants.
- **Ureases** catalyze the hydrolysis of urea into ammonia and carbon dioxide, a key step in nitrogen cycling, which is vital for plant growth.
- **Dehydrogenases** are involved in soil microbial respiration, which reflects the overall biological activity and fertility of the soil.

By supplementing soil with enzyme-based products, farmers can promote microbial activity, enhance nutrient availability, and reduce the dependency on synthetic fertilizers, leading to more sustainable agricultural practices.

20.2. Enzymes in Composting and Organic Matter Decomposition

Composting is a common agricultural practice that involves the decomposition of organic matter to produce nutrient-rich compost.

Enzymes are key players in this process, breaking down complex organic materials into simpler compounds that plants can readily absorb.

- **Cellulases** break down cellulose, a major component of plant cell walls, into glucose molecules.
- **Ligninases** degrade lignin, another component of plant biomass that is difficult to decompose.
- **Proteases** hydrolyze proteins in organic matter into amino acids, which can be utilized by plants and soil microorganisms.

The use of enzyme-based composting accelerates the breakdown of organic waste, leading to faster production of compost and improved soil structure. This method also reduces the need for chemical fertilizers and supports organic farming practices by enhancing soil organic matter.

20.3. Enzyme-Based Biopesticides

In recent years, enzymes have been employed as biopesticides to control pests and diseases in agriculture. These biopesticides are an eco-friendly alternative to synthetic chemicals, offering targeted pest control with minimal environmental impact.

- **Chitinases** break down chitin, a key component of the exoskeleton of insects and fungal cell walls. By degrading chitin, chitinase-based products can protect crops from fungal pathogens and insect pests.
- **Glucanases** degrade glucans, which are present in the cell walls of many plant pathogens. The application of glucanases can disrupt the growth of harmful fungi and bacteria, providing a biological defense against crop diseases.
- **Lipases** and **proteases** can also be used to disrupt the protective membranes of pests, weakening them and reducing their ability to damage crops.

These enzyme-based biopesticides offer a sustainable and safe alternative to conventional chemical pesticides, minimizing the risks to beneficial insects, soil health, and water ecosystems.

20.4. Enzymes in Animal Feed and Nutrition

Enzymes are increasingly used in livestock feed to improve nutrient digestibility and animal health. When added to animal feed, enzymes help break down complex nutrients that animals cannot digest on their own, enhancing nutrient absorption and reducing feed waste.

- **Phytases** break down phytic acid, a form of phosphorus that is not readily available to monogastric animals (such as poultry and swine). By degrading phytic acid, phytases increase the bioavailability of phosphorus, reducing the need for supplemental phosphorus in feed and lowering the environmental impact of phosphorus excretion.
- **Proteases** enhance protein digestion, allowing animals to utilize more of the dietary protein and improving growth performance.
- **Amylases** and **cellulases** aid in the breakdown of carbohydrates and fibers in feed, promoting better energy utilization and feed efficiency.

Enzyme supplementation in animal feed has become an essential tool in modern livestock management, optimizing feed efficiency, promoting animal health, and reducing the environmental footprint of livestock production.

20.5. Enzymes for Improving Plant Growth and Crop Yields

Enzymes are directly applied to crops to enhance plant growth, increase resilience to stress, and boost overall crop yields. Some enzyme formulations are designed to improve root development, enhance nutrient uptake, or stimulate the plant's natural defense mechanisms against pathogens.

- **Peroxidases** and **polyphenol oxidases** can activate the plant's defense response by inducing the production of antimicrobial compounds and strengthening cell walls.
- **Auxin-producing enzymes** promote root development, which enhances the plant's ability to absorb water and nutrients from the soil.
- **Amylases** are applied to seed treatments to break down starch reserves in seeds, improving germination rates and seedling vigor.

These enzyme treatments are used both as foliar sprays and soil amendments, offering a natural way to improve crop productivity without the need for chemical growth enhancers or fertilizers.

20.6. Enzymes in Agricultural Waste Management

Agricultural waste, such as crop residues, animal manure, and agro-industrial by-products, poses significant environmental challenges if not properly managed. Enzymes provide an effective solution for managing agricultural waste through bioconversion and waste degradation processes.

- **Lipases** and **proteases** help in breaking down organic wastes, such as fats and proteins, making them more biodegradable and easier to process.
- **Cellulases** and **hemicellulases** convert plant residues into biofuels or other value-added products, contributing to waste-to-energy initiatives in agriculture.

By using enzyme-based technologies, farmers can transform agricultural waste into valuable resources, reduce environmental pollution, and contribute to the circular economy.

20.7. Enzymes for Biofertilizer Production

Biofertilizers are microbial formulations that enhance soil fertility by fixing nitrogen, solubilizing phosphorus, and decomposing organic matter. Enzymes play a vital role in the production and action of biofertilizers by promoting the activity of beneficial microorganisms.

- **Nitrogenase enzymes** are produced by nitrogen-fixing bacteria and help convert atmospheric nitrogen into forms usable by plants, reducing the need for synthetic nitrogen fertilizers.
- **Phosphate-solubilizing enzymes** produced by microorganisms release insoluble phosphates in the soil, making them available for plant uptake.

The use of enzyme-enhanced biofertilizers supports sustainable agriculture by improving soil fertility, reducing chemical inputs, and promoting eco-friendly farming practices.

20.8. Enzymes in Crop Residue Management and Stubble Degradation

Managing crop residues, such as straw and stubble, is a major challenge in agriculture. Burning these residues leads to air pollution, while leaving them in fields can hinder planting for the next season. Enzymes can assist in the rapid degradation of crop residues, breaking down cellulose and lignin components and converting them into organic matter.

- **Ligninases** and **cellulases** help break down stubble left after harvest, accelerating the decomposition process and converting residues into valuable organic matter that can enrich the soil.

This enzymatic approach to crop residue management not only improves soil health but also reduces the need for harmful practices like residue burning.

The application of enzymes in agriculture presents significant advantages in terms of improving productivity, promoting sustainability, and reducing the environmental impact of farming practices. From enhancing soil fertility and nutrient availability to supporting biopesticides, waste management, and biofertilizer production, enzymes offer versatile solutions to the challenges faced by modern agriculture. As the demand for sustainable and eco-friendly farming grows, the use of enzymes in agriculture is likely to expand, paving the way for more efficient, productive, and resilient agricultural systems.

CHAPTER XXI

Emerging Trends in Enzyme Research

Emerging trends in enzyme research are revolutionizing the field by expanding the boundaries of enzyme applications, enhancing their performance, and unlocking new potentials for industrial, biomedical, and environmental uses. As the complexity of biological systems and the demands for innovative solutions continue to grow, enzyme research is increasingly focused on integrating cutting-edge technologies and interdisciplinary approaches. Advances in genomics and proteomics are driving the discovery of novel enzymes with unique properties and functions, while breakthroughs in structural biology provide deeper insights into enzyme mechanisms and interactions. The development of high-throughput screening and computational tools enables rapid characterization and optimization of enzyme variants, accelerating the pace of innovation. Additionally, the incorporation of nanotechnology and materials science is enhancing enzyme stability, activity, and specificity, leading to new applications in areas such as biocatalysis, biosensing, and environmental remediation. The exploration of synthetic biology and directed evolution is pushing the boundaries of enzyme engineering, allowing for the creation of custom-designed enzymes with tailored functions. Furthermore, the integration of artificial intelligence and machine learning is transforming how enzyme data is analysed and utilized, offering new avenues for predicting enzyme behaviour and optimizing enzyme-based processes. These emerging trends highlight a dynamic and rapidly evolving field that holds promise for addressing complex challenges and driving advancements across diverse sectors.

21.1 Directed Evolution:

Directed evolution represents a transformative approach in enzyme engineering that harnesses the principles of natural selection to create enzymes with tailored properties for a wide range of applications. This technique mimics the evolutionary process by generating a diverse library of enzyme variants through methods such as random mutagenesis and recombination. These variants are then subjected to rigorous screening or selection processes to identify those with desirable traits, such as enhanced activity, specificity, stability, or resistance to inhibitors. By iteratively applying selection pressures and introducing new mutations, directed evolution enables the fine-tuning of enzyme functions beyond the capabilities of natural enzymes. This method not only accelerates the optimization process but also allows for the exploration of previously inaccessible sequence and structural spaces. The power of directed evolution lies in its ability to adapt enzymes for various industrial, biomedical, and environmental applications, including biocatalysis, drug discovery, and environmental remediation. Its success is exemplified by numerous breakthroughs in enzyme engineering, where directed evolution has led to the development of highly effective biocatalysts and novel enzyme functionalities that were previously unattainable. As a dynamic and evolving field, directed evolution continues to drive innovation and expand the horizons of enzyme technology, offering unprecedented opportunities for solving complex challenges across multiple sectors. Here's a detailed overview:

21.1.1 Principles of Directed Evolution:

Directed evolution is founded on the concept of Darwinian evolution, where genetic diversity is introduced into enzyme populations, and variants with improved traits are selectively enriched through iterative rounds of mutagenesis, screening, and amplification. The key principles include:

21.1.1.1 Generation of Genetic Diversity:

Genetic diversity in enzyme libraries is often generated through random mutagenesis techniques such as error-prone PCR, DNA shuffling, and gene recombination. These methods introduce variations in the enzyme's genetic code, which can lead to alterations in enzyme structure and function. Mutations may be targeted to specific regions of the enzyme gene, where critical activity-related residues are located, or distributed randomly throughout the coding sequence to explore a broader range of sequence space. This approach allows researchers to explore different enzyme variants, optimizing or discovering new catalytic activities that could have applications in various fields such as biotechnology, agriculture, and medicine. Generating genetic diversity is a foundational step in directed evolution, where these enzyme variants are screened for improved or novel functions.

21.1.1.2 Selection or Screening:

After generating genetic diversity in enzyme libraries, the next crucial step is selection or screening, where engineered enzyme variants are tested to identify those with the desired traits. This process typically involves high-throughput screening or selection assays to evaluate various functional properties such as enzyme activity, substrate specificity, stability, or other relevant attributes for the intended application. Screening assays may involve measuring reaction rates or changes in product formation to detect improvements in enzyme performance. Selection methods often apply selective pressures, such as exposure to substrate analogues, temperature extremes, pH variations, or solvent conditions, to enrich for enzyme variants that exhibit enhanced functionality under specific environmental conditions. This step allows researchers to sift through a large number of variants efficiently, isolating the most promising candidates for further analysis or optimization.

21.1.1.3 Iterative Cycles of Evolution:

Once promising enzyme variants are selected, they are isolated and thoroughly characterized to assess their improved traits. These selected variants then undergo further rounds of mutagenesis and screening in an iterative process to refine and enhance enzyme properties. This cyclic process, known as directed evolution, allows for incremental improvements in performance by introducing new beneficial mutations in each round. Over successive cycles, the enzyme's activity, stability, substrate specificity, or other desired traits are progressively optimized, resulting in enzymes tailored to specific applications or conditions. Directed evolution is a powerful method for developing highly efficient and specialized biocatalysts.

21.1.2 Applications of Directed Evolution:

Directed evolution has broad applications across various industrial and biomedical fields, including:

21.1.2.1 Biocatalysis:

Directed evolution is widely employed to optimize enzyme catalysts for industrial biocatalysis, where enzymes are engineered for specific applications such as the synthesis of fine chemicals, pharmaceutical intermediates, and specialty compounds. By improving key enzyme traits—such as catalytic activity, selectivity, and stability—engineered enzymes offer significant advantages over traditional chemical catalysts. These enhanced biocatalysts provide a more cost-effective and environmentally friendly solution, reducing the need for harsh chemicals and extreme conditions in industrial processes. This makes directed evolution a crucial tool in advancing sustainable and efficient biotechnological manufacturing.

21.1.2.2 Biosensing:

Directed evolution is harnessed to develop enzyme-based biosensors used for detecting environmental pollutants, pathogens, biomarkers, or therapeutic drug levels in clinical samples. By engineering enzymes with enhanced sensitivity, specificity, or faster response kinetics, biosensors become more accurate and reliable for diagnostic and analytical applications. These optimized enzymes allow for the detection of trace amounts of harmful substances or critical biological markers, making them valuable in environmental monitoring, medical diagnostics, and pharmaceutical research, where precision and rapid response are essential.

21.1.2.3 Drug Discovery:

Directed evolution plays a crucial role in engineering enzymes for drug discovery and development processes, encompassing enzyme targets for drug screening assays, enzyme inhibitors for therapeutic interventions, and biocatalysts for pharmaceutical synthesis. By generating enzymes with novel or enhanced catalytic activities, scientists can synthesize drug-like molecules, discover new lead compounds, and optimize drug candidates for better pharmacological properties. This approach accelerates the development of effective therapies by enabling precise control over enzyme functions, improving drug efficacy, and reducing production costs in pharmaceutical synthesis.

21.1.2.4 Environmental Remediation:

Directed evolution significantly advances the development of enzymes for environmental remediation applications, including the degradation of persistent pollutants, detoxification of industrial waste streams, and production of renewable biofuels. By engineering enzymes with improved activity or substrate specificity, scientists can create more efficient and sustainable solutions for addressing environmental challenges. These advanced enzymes provide eco-friendly alternatives to traditional chemical treatments, enhancing the ability to mitigate pollution and reduce environmental impact through biocatalysis.

Directed evolution is a versatile and powerful approach in enzyme engineering, enabling the customization of enzymes with desired properties for a wide range of industrial, biomedical, and environmental applications. By harnessing the principles of natural evolution, directed evolution accelerates the discovery and optimization of enzymes for diverse biotechnological and therapeutic purposes, driving innovation and sustainability in various fields.Top of Form

21.2. Enzyme Engineering:

Enzyme engineering represents a multifaceted approach to tailoring enzyme properties to meet the specific needs of industrial, biomedical, and environmental applications. By leveraging a combination of molecular biology, biochemistry, and advanced computational tools, enzyme engineering aims to modify and optimize enzymes to enhance their performance, stability, and specificity for targeted functions. This approach involves a variety of techniques, including site-directed mutagenesis, directed evolution, and rational design, which collectively enable the creation of enzymes with improved catalytic activity, altered substrate preferences, and enhanced resistance to harsh conditions. In industrial contexts, enzyme engineering is employed to develop catalysts that drive more efficient and sustainable chemical processes, from manufacturing fine chemicals to producing renewable biofuels. In the biomedical field, engineered enzymes are used to create diagnostic tools, therapeutic agents, and drug delivery systems with enhanced efficacy and safety profiles. Environmental applications benefit from enzyme engineering through the development of biocatalysts that address pollution and waste management challenges. Overall, enzyme engineering is a dynamic and evolving discipline that plays a critical role in advancing technology and addressing complex challenges across various sectors, driving innovation and contributing to the development of sustainable solutions for global issues. Here's a comprehensive overview of enzyme engineering techniques and their applications:

21.2.1. Rational Design:

Rational design is a strategic approach to enzyme engineering that involves the precise modification of enzyme structure and function, guided by a thorough understanding of protein structure, catalytic mechanisms, and substrate interactions. This technique relies on advanced methods such as site-directed mutagenesis, protein modelling, and structural analysis to introduce targeted mutations or alterations into enzyme sequences. By focusing on specific areas of the enzyme's structure, rational design aims to enhance various properties, including catalytic efficiency, substrate specificity, thermal stability, pH tolerance, and resistance to inhibitors. These improvements are crucial for optimizing enzymes for diverse biotechnological applications, including biocatalysis, biosensing, and drug discovery. Rational design enables the development of enzymes with tailored characteristics to meet the demands of specific industrial processes, diagnostic tools, and therapeutic agents, contributing to advancements in science and technology.

21.2.2. Semi-Rational Design:

Semi-rational design represents an advanced approach to enzyme engineering that combines computational modelling with experimental validation to guide the optimization of enzyme properties. This methodology integrates the predictive power of computational algorithms with empirical data to enhance enzyme performance. Techniques used in semi-rational design include molecular docking, molecular dynamics simulations, and homology modelling, which help predict the effects of mutations on enzyme structure and function. By leveraging these computational tools, semi-rational design accelerates the exploration of sequence and structural space, facilitating more efficient optimization of enzyme properties. This approach streamlines the identification of promising enzyme variants, which can then be subjected to directed evolution or further experimental validation. The semi rational design approach significantly enhances the efficiency of enzyme engineering projects, leading to the development of enzymes with tailored properties for diverse applications in biocatalysis, biosensing, and other biotechnological fields.

21.2.3. Directed Evolution:

Directed evolution is a powerful and versatile approach in enzyme engineering that leverages iterative rounds of random mutagenesis, screening, and selection to develop enzyme variants with enhanced or novel functions. This technique involves the introduction of genetic diversity into enzyme libraries through methods such as error-prone PCR, DNA shuffling, or recombination. Once a diverse pool of enzyme variants is generated, high-throughput screening or selection assays are employed to identify those with desired traits. Directed evolution is particularly valuable for optimizing enzyme properties such as activity, substrate specificity, and stability, making it applicable across a wide range of biotechnological fields. This includes biocatalysis for industrial processes, biosensing for environmental and clinical diagnostics, drug discovery for identifying novel therapeutic targets, and environmental remediation for tackling pollution and waste management challenges. Through its iterative and empirical nature, directed evolution facilitates the creation of tailored enzymes that meet specific application needs, driving advances in technology and science.

21.2.4. High-Throughput Screening (HTS):

High-throughput screening (HTS) methods are crucial for the rapid and efficient evaluation of large enzyme libraries to identify variants with desirable properties. These techniques leverage advanced automated platforms, microfluidic devices, and robotic systems to simultaneously screen thousands to millions of enzyme variants, measuring various functional parameters such as enzymatic activity, substrate specificity, or stability. By enabling the parallel assessment of extensive libraries, HTS accelerates the identification and characterization of superior enzyme candidates derived from directed evolution, rational design, or semi-rational design approaches. This rapid evaluation process is essential for advancing the development of tailored enzymes suited for specific industrial, biomedical, or environmental applications. As a result, HTS plays a pivotal role in enhancing enzyme engineering efforts, streamlining the pathway from enzyme discovery to practical application.

21.3. Nanotechnology and Enzymes:

Nanotechnology has rapidly emerged as a transformative field with the potential to revolutionize enzyme technology by integrating enzymes with nanomaterials. This convergence of disciplines offers unprecedented opportunities to enhance enzyme functionality and application across various domains. At the heart of this synergy is the ability of nanomaterials to influence and modify the properties of enzymes, resulting in improved stability, activity, and specificity. Nanotechnology enables the creation of enzyme-nanomaterial composites that can enhance enzyme performance under harsh conditions, such as extreme temperatures or varying pH levels, which are often challenging for traditional enzyme applications. Additionally, the unique properties of nanomaterials, such as their high surface area-to-volume ratio and customizable surface chemistry, facilitate the development of highly efficient and targeted enzyme systems. This integration also paves the way for advanced biosensing and diagnostic platforms, where nanomaterials can amplify signal detection and improve sensitivity. By harnessing the capabilities of nanotechnology, researchers and engineers are pushing the boundaries of enzyme technology, leading to innovations in industrial processes, environmental applications, and medical diagnostics. This fusion of nanotechnology and enzymology promises to unlock new possibilities and drive significant advancements in both fields.

Here's a detailed exploration of the intersection between nanotechnology and enzymes:

21.3.1. Nanostructured Enzyme Materials:

Nanostructured enzyme materials represent a cutting-edge integration of enzymes with nanoscale structures, where enzymes are either immobilized, encapsulated, or supported on various nanomaterials such as nanoparticles, nanofibers, nanotubes, or nanosheets. This innovative approach leverages the unique properties of nanomaterials to enhance the functionality and performance of enzymes. The incorporation of enzymes into nanostructures offers several significant advantages: improved stability, which allows enzymes to retain their activity under harsh conditions like high temperatures or extreme pH levels; enhanced reusability, enabling the recovery and reuse of enzymes in continuous processes; and an increased surface area-to-volume ratio that enhances catalytic efficiency. These nanostructured enzyme materials are employed in a wide range of applications, including biocatalysis, where they catalyze industrial chemical reactions more efficiently; biosensing, where they improve the sensitivity and specificity of detection assays; drug delivery, where they enable targeted and controlled release of therapeutic agents; and environmental remediation, where they help in the breakdown of pollutants. The development and application of nanostructured enzyme materials highlight the transformative potential of nanotechnology in advancing enzyme technology and addressing complex challenges across various fields.

21.3.2. Bionanocomposites:

Bionanocomposites represent an innovative class of hybrid materials created by integrating enzymes with nanomaterials to harness synergistic effects that enhance both structural and functional properties. These composites leverage the unique attributes of both components—enzymes and nanomaterials—to develop materials with superior performance. The combination of enzymes with nanomaterials results in improved catalytic performance, heightened substrate selectivity, and increased stability of the enzymes, while also potentially enhancing the biocompatibility of the composite. The synergistic effects of bionanocomposites enable their application across a broad spectrum of fields. In biomedical diagnostics, they are used to develop highly sensitive and specific assays for detecting biomarkers or pathogens. In therapeutics, bionanocomposites facilitate targeted drug delivery and controlled release of therapeutic agents. Their role in tissue engineering includes promoting cell growth and tissue repair.

In biocatalysis, these composites offer improved efficiency for industrial chemical reactions. Additionally, bionanocomposites find uses in food technology for improving food processing and preservation, and in environmental monitoring and remediation for detecting and degrading pollutants. The integration of enzymes with nanomaterials in bionanocomposites exemplifies the potential of nanotechnology to create advanced materials with enhanced capabilities and diverse applications.

21.3.3. Nanobiocatalysis:

Nanobiocatalysis represents a cutting-edge approach that leverages nanomaterials to modulate and enhance enzyme activity, substrate interactions, and reaction kinetics, offering precise control over enzymatic processes. By integrating nanomaterials with enzymes, nanobiocatalysis introduces a range of functionalities that significantly impact enzymatic reactions. Nanomaterials can serve various roles, such as scaffolds that provide structural support, carriers that facilitate enzyme delivery, or regulators that influence enzyme behavior. These materials offer benefits such as spatial confinement of enzymes, which can lead to enhanced mass transfer and improved stability, as well as the creation of controlled microenvironments that optimize reaction conditions. The principles of nanobiocatalysis enable advancements across multiple applications. In biosensing, nanobiocatalysis enhances the sensitivity and specificity of diagnostic assays. For bioremediation, it improves the efficiency of enzyme-based degradation of environmental pollutants. In biomanufacturing and fine chemical synthesis, nanobiocatalysis contributes to more efficient and selective production processes. The pharmaceutical industry benefits from nanobiocatalysis through the development of novel drug synthesis methods, while renewable energy technologies utilize these innovations to improve biofuel production and other sustainable energy solutions. The integration of nanomaterials with enzymatic systems through nanobiocatalysis exemplifies the transformative potential of nanotechnology in optimizing and expanding the capabilities of enzymatic processes.

These emerging trends in enzyme research demonstrate the evolving landscape of enzyme technology, from directed evolution and enzyme engineering to the integration of enzymes with nanomaterials. These advancements hold promise for developing innovative solutions to address challenges in biotechnology, medicine, and environmental science, paving the way for the next generation of enzyme-based technologies.

Author Bio

Dr. Jitendra Kumar

Dr. Jitendra Kumar holds a B.Sc. in Zoology, Botany, and Chemistry from Dr. Bhimrao Ambedkar University, and an M.Sc. in Biotechnology and Ph.D. in Genetics and Plant Breeding from Chaudhary Charan Singh University. With over 4 years of research and teaching experience, he has published more than 20 papers in reputed national and international journals. Dr. Kumar has qualified prestigious exams including GATE, ICMR-JRF, and ASRB-NET, and has received several accolades, such as the Best Poster Award at IARI in 2016 and the Scientist Associate Award at a national conference in Hyderabad. He has participated in over 15 national and international conferences and workshops. Currently, Dr. Kumar is an SERB National Post-Doctoral Fellow at the National Agri-Food Biotechnology Institute (NABI), Mohali, India.

Co-author Bio

Shoeb Ahmed

Shoeb Ahmed holds a B.Sc. and M.Sc. in Biotechnology, along with a B.Ed., and has over 10 years of teaching experience. He has qualified prestigious exams such as GATE, CSIR-UGC NET-JRF, CTET, and UPTET, demonstrating his expertise in the field of education and biotechnology. With a passion for teaching and mentoring, Shoeb has been committed to shaping future minds in science and education.

Declaration

We hereby declare that the book titled *Exploring Enzyme: Nature's Catalyst* is an original work authored with the sole purpose of introducing the basics of enzymology to undergraduate students. This book has been carefully developed to provide a comprehensive yet accessible understanding of enzyme science, drawing upon established knowledge in the field while presenting it in a clear and simplified manner for educational purposes.

All content, including text, illustrations, and explanations, is a product of my research and understanding of the subject matter. Any similarity to existing work is purely coincidental and unintentional. We affirm that this book does not plagiarize any existing material, and any resemblance to previously published work is coincidental. Should any overlap be identified, it is entirely coincidental and will be addressed accordingly.

Author: **Dr. Jitendra Kumar**

Co-Author: **Shoeb Ahmed**

www.ingramcontent.com/pod-product-compliance
Lightning Source LLC
Chambersburg PA
CBHW040741120726
48007CB00007B/49